J. K. ROWLING

A Biography

Connie Ann Kirk

GREENWOOD BIOGRAPHIES

GREENWOOD PRESS
WESTPORT, CONNECTICUT · LONDON

Library of Congress Cataloging-in-Publication Data

Kirk, Connie Ann.
   J.K. Rowling : a biography / Connie Ann Kirk.
      p. cm.—(Greenwood biographies, ISSN 1540–4900)
   Includes bibliographical references and index.
   ISBN 0–313–32205–8 (alk. paper)
   1. Rowling, J. K. 2. Authors, English—20th century—Biography. 3. Potter, Harry (Fic-
titious character) 4. Children's stories—Authorship. I. Title: Joanne K. Rowling. II. Title.
III. Series.

PR6068.O93 Z739 2003
823′.914—dc21
[B]   2002075330

British Library Cataloguing in Publication Data is available.

Library of Congress Catalog Card Number: 2002075330
ISBN: 0–313–32205–8
ISSN: 1540–4900

First published in 2003

Greenwood Press, 88 Post Road West, Westport, CT 06881
An imprint of Greenwood Publishing Group, Inc.
www.greenwood.com

Printed in the United States of America

The paper used in this book complies with the
Permanent Paper Standard issued by the National
Information Standards Organization (Z39.48–1984).

10 9 8 7 6 5 4 3 2

to Ben and John,
the wizards of my heart

CONTENTS

Photo essay follows chapter 4

SERIES FOREWORD

In response to high school and public library needs, Greenwood developed this distinguished series of full-length biographies specifically for student use. Prepared by field experts and professionals, these engaging biographies are tailored for high school students who need challenging yet accessible biographies. Ideal for secondary school assignments, the length, format and subject areas are designed to meet educators' requirements and students' interests.

Greenwood offers an extensive selection of biographies spanning all curriculum-related subject areas including social studies, the sciences, literature and the arts, history and politics, as well as popular culture, covering public figures and famous personalities from all time periods and backgrounds, both historic and contemporary, who have made an impact on American and/or world culture. Greenwood biographies were chosen based on comprehensive feedback from librarians and educators. Consideration was given to both curriculum relevance and inherent interest. The result is an intriguing mix of the well known and the unexpected, the saints and sinners from long-ago history and contemporary pop culture. Readers will find a wide array of subject choices from fascinating crime figures like Al Capone to inspiring pioneers like Margaret Mead, from the greatest minds of our time like Stephen Hawking to the most amazing success stories of our day like J.K. Rowling.

While the emphasis is on fact, not glorification, the books are meant to be fun to read. Each volume provides in-depth information about the subject's life from birth through childhood, the teen years, and adulthood. A thorough account relates family background and education, traces personal and professional influences, and explores struggles, accomplishments, and contributions. A timeline highlights the most significant life events against a historical perspective. Suggestions for further reading give the biographies added reference value.

PREFACE

To those living around me while I was working on this project, I have frequently described the challenge of writing a biography about a living author in the prime of her life and at the height of her career as something like chasing a tornado. The subject is continually changing and moving at top speed (she is a living, breathing human being, after all), and the details about her life keep getting swept up and spit out as quickly as the information is gathered and verified or proven false. Trying to write an accurate story from a dizzying sea of misinformation about a subject fighting to keep her private life private amid the blitz of a massive popular culture environment at times seemed to be an almost impossible task; however, the reader should know that a sincere effort has been made here, just the same.

As yet, there is no full-length scholarly biography of J.K. Rowling in existence, so that makes writing a biography for the general reader and education audience even more challenging in terms of gathering and evaluating information. My mode of working has been to cast a wide net. I obtained every biography that was in print, watched or read a transcript of every live or taped interview I could find, then went deep sea fishing in the dangerous waters of the internet. Wherever possible, I yielded to Jo Rowling's own accounts of events. Sometimes, to my surprise, even she appeared to contradict herself, such as when she said in one interview that she did not particularly care for fantasies, and then in other places she mentions reading a number of them, even placing fantasies such as Elizabeth Goudge's *The Little White Horse* among her favorite books as a child. For a biographer, even one who is trying to gather information for the interested general reader as well as for students and teachers to use in the classroom, details like this are frustrating, to say the least. I hope my sincere attempt to relay the information as I found it and was best able to evaluate it at the time will be considered when new and conflicting information comes along, as it inevitably will.

I want to thank Sean Smith for his very helpful book, *J.K. Rowling: A Biography*, which came out just when I needed a rudder to help guide this biography written for Greenwood's author series. Despite the faults that some have found with it, including Rowling's own reported dismissal, Smith's mass market book is the best documented, most thorough, and fairest treatment of J.K. Rowling's life that I have seen to date, and much of the information I include in this volume I owe to Smith's well-meaning work. I applaud his effort to clarify some inconsistencies in previously reported information (for example, he includes a copy of Rowling's birth certificate in his book that contradicts Rowling's statement of where she was born) and for interviewing many of the people in Rowling's life, even if, for the most part, they are not what readers might call the "main characters," such as family and closest friends. Inconsistencies and challenged information still exist, nonetheless, and I hope readers of this book will feel free to contact the author through Greenwood to offer corrections and additions for subsequent editions. Famous as she is, J.K. Rowling is still a relatively new author, and information about her life remains sketchy and incomplete.

I would also like to thank Lindsey Fraser for her work, which I also used as source material for this one. Ms. Fraser interviewed Rowling for the two autobiographical books that have appeared thus far—in the United States *Conversations with J.K. Rowling,* published by Scholastic, and in England *An Interview with J.K. Rowling,* part of the Telling Tales series published by Mammoth. Without the trust that Ms. Fraser has obviously engendered from Jo Rowling, we would perhaps not have Rowling's own words in book form answering many of the most frequently asked questions from general readers, teachers, and students about her life and her writing. Wherever possible, I have deferred to Rowling's own answers to questions that come up about her biography.

Philip Nel's *J.K. Rowling's Harry Potter Novels: A Reader's Guide,* part of the Continuum Contemporaries series published by Continuum, provides a good, quick introduction to the novels from a literary point of view, especially in terms of the novels' contexts within world literature. While the biography section in Nel's guide repeats several errors present in the earlier information circulated about the novelist, such as her birthdate, the guide does provide an adequate introduction to Rowling's placement thus far within various literary traditions.

By far the best reference I encountered for in-depth details about the novels themselves within the realm of Rowling's made-up world is the "Harry Potter Lexicon," edited and maintained on the web by librarian Steve Vander Ark at http://www.i2k.com/~svderark/lexicon/index.html. Vander Ark's work in compiling plot timelines, lists of language variations between the British and American publications, and various other lists and information was a good resource for questions of that sort that came up occasionally in my work.

The last resource for this project that I'd like to recognize here is the biographical documentary made with Rowling's cooperation, "J. K. Rowling: Harry Potter and Me," originally broadcast by the British Broadcasting Company (BBC) in late 2001 and re-aired in the United States on the Arts & Entertainment (A&E) network as an A&E *Biography* program in 2002. In the documentary, Rowling relates facts about her own story on location from the various places of importance to her life and work and clarifies some widespread misconceptions. The documentary contains information that older readers, the audience for which this book is intended, will find especially interesting.

I would like to thank Lynn Malloy at Greenwood, who initiated the idea for a general reader and education biography and asked me to write it. Thanks also to Ms. Rowling's agent, Christopher Little, and her American editor, Arthur A. Levine, for their gracious and helpful replies to my requests for information.

A special personal thank you to my family—Ken, Ben and John—for living with, and taking an active interest in, this uninvited guest in our home for the duration of its research and writing. Finally, a last thank you to Jo Rowling, fellow traveler, for continuing to live her life with courage, cleverness, and a little help from her friends.

Chapter 1

ORIGINS AND CONTEXTS

It is early November 2001, and J.K. Rowling (pronounced "rolling") stands outside, posing for photos behind three young British actors. Flash-bulbs fire and pop every which way, and the author shows her characteristic closed-mouth grin while protectively touching the shoulders of the small actors in front of her. She's been through this before. Well, not quite, but she's certainly seen hype surrounding her books before. A year earlier she read to an audience of 12,000 people at Skydome Stadium in Toronto, Canada, an event that was quite possibly the largest audience recorded for an author's reading. She read before another 10,000 at the International Writers and Readers Festival in Vancouver just 24 hours later. She has appeared on American national television shows such as *The Today Show* and *Larry King Live,* which broadcast to millions of people every day. In England, she rode on a 57-year-old train for a four-day tour from King's Cross Station in London to meet with thousands of screaming fans hoping to obtain a coveted autograph. She watched in dismay, attempting to greet them, as her promoters forced her to stay onboard, waving from her compartment window and moving on with the rush of the promotional machinery to the next scheduled stops. In a single day's appearance in Boston in 1999, the fans lined up, curling around the block, and she signed 1,400 copies of her book. Just as her character, Harry Potter, woke up one day to find that he was famous in the wizard world, Jo Rowling must have found herself in a similar state of shock not long after her first book was published.

Her understanding of Harry must be growing by the day. While she admits a likeness to her own youth can be found in the book-loving character

Hermione, her life right now is more like Harry's—a reluctant, brave hero trying to do good with the new powers she is discovering she has had all along. The more power she gains in fame, influence, and wealth, the more her privacy and personal history are tread upon and the more those who desire what she has obtained try to undercut her success. Like Harry, her courage through some of the worst moments in her life provides the legends that propel fascination with her life now, even though those are times that left scars she'd often rather not be reminded of.

By mid-2002, the Harry Potter books had sold over 150 million copies and had been translated into more than 50 different languages—only the Bible has been translated into more. At its American release, the Warner Brothers film adaptation of *Harry Potter and the Sorcerer's Stone* grossed a record-breaking $31.3 million on opening day, blasting to another record-breaking $90.3 million over its opening three-day weekend. The film spurred another round of sales for the first book in the series, pushing it above the other three on the bestseller lists, which none of them has left since their publication. Sales of the video and DVD versions of the first film were also exceptional, even as they coincided with already popular computer games based on the story. Merchandising—including Harry Potter Legos, Harry Potter action figures, play sets, stationery, and clothing—boosted holiday sales in an otherwise dipping economy. Internet sites with Harry Potter's and Rowling's names yielded more than 1,800,000 hits.

The books are not just a popular and commercial success, either. There are more than a dozen books of literary criticism, reading companions, teaching guides, biographies, and other related studies already in print, with more on the way. Scholars of literature and popular culture are discussing the books and the aura of hype surrounding them, called "Pottermania" or the "Harry Potter Phenomenon," at academic conferences and in journal articles for the serious-minded. Professors are offering seminars on Harry Potter to upper-level college undergraduates. So far, the books have been praised more than they have been criticized in most circles, but negative criticism is growing in literary and education communities, especially in the form of backlash against commercialism caused by the films. All this, with only a bit more than half of the seven-part series in publication in 2002. The power of magic draws suspicion today as it always has, and the power of the imagination remains as mysterious as the power of magic.

The mirror of desire reflects the rags-to-riches story of Harry Potter over and over. Harry himself goes from rags to riches, and so does his creator, Jo Rowling. Daniel Radcliffe, the young actor from Liverpool who plays Harry in the first two feature films, is also undergoing a magical transformation to new found, worldwide fame. With Radcliffe just twelve years old at the time of the premiere of the first film, it is no wonder that Rowling reached out protectively behind him in the face of the barrage of photographers. She and Daniel share the same birthday, July 31, with the character they both hold dear in a way not even the most serious reader and dedicated fan will ever know. Other comparisons between Rowling and Radcliffe come to mind. Jo's and Daniel's eyes are similarly shaped; he could be her son based on their physical appearance. The actress in the movie who plays Lily Potter, Harry's mother, in the Mirror of Erised has the long reddish hair that is suggestive of Jo's in earlier days. In many ways, the stories of Jo, Harry, and Daniel are linked. Over time, we shall see how their stories unbraid and rebraid with one another. But this is Jo's story, and it is in her story that Harry's begins and Daniel's converges.

This book narrates the story beginning soon after the release of the first Harry Potter film by Warner Brothers in late 2001 and the release of the video and DVD in May, 2002. It then traces Jo Rowling's childhood and family life, moving gradually forward to her years in school, her early career, and then to the accounts of how Harry Potter originated in Rowling's imagination, the circumstances surrounding the completion and publishing history of the books, and finally the controversies that have arisen regarding the four books that have appeared to date.

How did a middle class, unemployed teacher from England who was down on her luck at the end of the twentieth century become one of the wealthiest women in Great Britain by the turn of the twenty-first century? What makes the Harry Potter books so popular around the world? How is J.K. Rowling holding up under the pressure of fame and promotional tours for the books and the films thus far? What is she doing with the mounting fortune that has come with the fame? What and who influenced Jo's life and career?

Over the course of this book, we shall try to identify and define some of the answers to these questions and others. Every attempt has been made to present the facts as they are currently known, in an as objective a way as possible. Discrepancies in information will be noted so that the reader may make up his/her own mind about areas in question or do further research from the continuing updates available on the story of this living person at the height of her career.

While every effort has been made to present information objectively, the author admits that biographies are not free from bias. Information must be validated and cross-checked for accuracy and evaluated for bias in terms of its source, but it is the biographer's decision whether or not to include validated material in the telling of a life story. The criteria on which decisions are made about leaving in or taking out information reflect a biographer's bias. This biographer admits the following biases up front, stemming from her own background: the perspective is distinctly American, moderately feminist, and reflects the sensibilities and interests of a fellow writer as well as a scholar of literature. These biases should be taken into consideration when evaluating claims made within this book.

With three volumes of the planned seven-book series yet to be published, it is perhaps unfair or premature to determine Jo Rowling's place as an author and contextualize her Harry Potter series within the vast universe of world literature. However, there are a few traditions and families of fiction with which the Harry Potter books appear to share commonalities, and these are worth noting, even at this stage in the series' publication. While Jo Rowling has said that she is writing the Harry Potter books for her own pleasure and amusement as an adult, most readers acknowledge that the books gained their initial fame as children's books. Within the constellation of children's books, the series can be compared with others in a number of ways. There are many children's series in which the same core group of characters appear in most or all of the books. Laura Ingalls Wilder's Little House novels, for example, are autobiographical accounts of Laura Ingalls's family life growing up on the plains of the midwestern United States. The series shares the same group of characters, with some additions and deletions as the narratives move forward in time, age, and maturity. Popular "whodunnits" or detective series for children and young adults such as The Hardy Boys and Nancy Drew share a common set of characters grouped as friends or relatives who solve mysteries in novel after novel. The Oz books by L. Frank Baum, and Beatrix Potter's Peter Rabbit books are others. One difference between series of this type and Rowling's is that each book is an independent story, not necessarily a continuation of a number of tightly woven plot lines, as the Harry Potter books are. Also, many series books, such as the Stratemeyer Syndicate books, The Hardy Boys and Nancy Drew, become a commercial franchise that gets taken over by other authors when the original author dies, thus diminishing the authenticity of the original stories. Rowling has said that she has planned out all seven of the books in her series very carefully and that the series will end with book seven. She has even written the series epilogue, which will explain what happens to all of the remaining Harry Potter characters after they leave Hogwarts School of Witchcraft and Wizardry.

A category of children's books that has a strong claim to the Harry Potter books is the genre of fantasy fiction. Fantasy includes a made-up world which, with children's books in particular, usually involves animals or animal-like creatures that exhibit human-like qualities. Inanimate objects may also come to life with personalities of their own. Probably some of the best-known fantasies for children include Kenneth Grahame's *The Wind in the Willows*; C.S. Lewis's *Chronicles of Narnia*; Philip Pullman's series, including *The Golden Compass*; E.B. White's *Charlotte's Web*, *Stuart Little*, and *The Trumpet of the Swan*; Lewis Carroll's *The Adventures of Alice in Wonderland*, and Beatrix Potter's Peter Rabbit books, as well as J.R.R. Tolkien's *The Hobbit* and *The Lord of the Rings* trilogy.

Fantasy allows the writer to create an entire world and populate it with whatever kind of flora and fauna and characters she or he desires. The boundaries seem almost limitless in these made-up worlds, but the author must know that boundaries exist within all worlds in order for the settings to be fully formed and believable. Readers of fantasy enjoy the freedom from the world they know but recognize and expect to learn the limits of the new world created by the fantasy writer. Part of the enjoyment of reading fantasy is pushing the limits with the author, learning right alongside the characters what is and isn't possible in this strange and unusual place, then coming to grips with how this setting is alike and different from the world we do know.

School stories are another longstanding tradition that the Harry Potter books share with the category of children's literature. School stories are set in academia or have plots that revolve around specific school settings and include an emphasis on school friendships and conflicts with teachers and/or schoolwork. Often there are social problems with bullies on the playground that a more sensitive character must confront. School-sponsored sporting events frequently provide a setting for climactic scenes where conflicts that have arisen elsewhere are played out in a safe environment. In Britain, many novels in this genre open and close with train rides to boarding schools. The first known British novel in the school story genre is *Tom Brown's Schooldays* by Thomas Hughes, published in 1857. The novel initiated the now-familiar motifs of school stories of its kind, which stopped being produced in large numbers between the world wars in the twentieth century. Motifs include a boy protagonist in boarding school, a kindly headmaster but some questionable teachers, school bullies, school sports championship tournaments, and experiences of self-discovery for the hero.

A third genre that can lay claim to the Harry Potter series within children's literature—or more properly its older sibling, young adult or adolescent literature—is the coming-of-age story. This is more evident in the later Harry Potter books, and when all of the books are considered together this will perhaps be an even more prominent theme. Books of this sort describe a character's maturation from childhood to adulthood, from innocence to experience, from naiveté to knowledge. Coming-of-age books have been popular for a long time and include classics such as J.D. Salinger's *The Catcher in the Rye* and Sylvia Plath's *The Bell Jar*, as well as more recent titles such as Karen Hesse's *Out of the Dust*. Usually, these stories involve introducing the main character to a complex, adult situation. The conflict and how the protagonist deals with it result in growth and maturation of the adolescent and propel him/her toward adulthood. Readers of coming-of-age books must be sensitive about when they are ready to read about some of these complex, adult issues. In more recent years, the issues that shape these books have gone beyond the death of a loved one or the struggle between good and evil to other problems that are perhaps even more complicated. Young adult issues include war, disease, crime, dysfunctional families, alcoholism and other substance abuse, eating disorders, and complex social issues such as abortion, sexual activity, sexual orientation, sexually transmitted diseases such as AIDS, euthanasia, and poverty and injustice. Readers of the first four Harry Potter books have said that they are curious about what issues Harry may confront at Hogwarts in the latter books, which even Rowling has admitted are perhaps more appropriate for an adolescent audience. Many readers sense a foreshadowed deepening of the series' complexity beginning in book four.

The Harry Potter novels are also very popular with adults, and their connection to various genres in adult fiction makes it easy to see that there are several precedents to suggest that this would be the case. Among fantasies, Rowling's series is most often compared to J.R.R. Tolkien's trilogy, *The Lord of the Rings*, which she has admitted to reading. Rowling has pointed out that Tolkien created a much more elaborate alternative world—a Middle Earth complete with not only different beings, societies, and plants and animals as she has done, but also with its own languages and myths, which Tolkien worked out in intricate detail. Tolkien created over a dozen new languages and alphabets in such detail that dedicated readers have actually studied them and have been able to speak and write using them. For the film release of the first book in the Tolkien trilogy in late 2001, the actors consulted with these experts to learn how to pronounce the made-up languages correctly.

Another school of fiction for adults that Rowling's books fit into is that involving orphan protagonists and benefactors, a tradition that Rowling inherits from her famous predecessor and countryman Charles Dickens. Interestingly, Dickens's well-known classics, such as *David Copperfield* and *Great Expectations*, were first serialized in periodicals that were wildly popular in their day. Dickens was a nineteenth-century British "celebrity" to be sure, one who was asked to give readings and was plied with questions from the public about what his popular characters were going to do in up-coming installments of the stories. Scholars admit that Dickens's writing in later installments was probably influenced by his readers' comments about earlier installments. Rowling has made a pledge to herself not to let this happen, since she has said she has all seven books already plotted out the way she wants the full story to go. Orphans also appear with great regularity, of course, in children's literature as well. It is a frequent technique to give the child protagonist more control in the plot.

Still another genre in both the adult and children's realm is that of logic puzzles and whodunits that require deductive reasoning to figure out questions or mysteries of the plot. Usually the reader can share in solving the puzzles with the same clues, but can also wait and follow along until the characters solve them. Games, both actual games like chess and made-up games of fantastic sorts, are also popular in many of these books. Books of this type include Lewis Carroll's *Through the Looking Glass* and Sir Arthur Conan Doyle's Sherlock Holmes series. Ellen Raskin's *The Westing Game* represents another children's version of this same genre.

It is not possible to say at this stage whether or not the Harry Potter series will have long-lasting appeal as great literature. Many readers see the series having that potential, given the many allusions to mythology and languages, the incredible popularity of the books, and the insatiable appetite for the books yet to be released in the series. They see generations of young readers growing up with the series year by year and book by book, establishing a relationship with the author and her characters that will outlive the feature films, commercialization, and bestseller lists. Some fans foresee this generation of children as having a strong desire to share this experience with their own children, thus keeping the Harry Potter series viable and relevant for a new generation of children. They point to the word-of-mouth popularity among kids that sparked the sales of the first books, and to the thousands of reluctant readers across the globe who have been initiated into the joy of reading through the Harry Potter series.

Skeptics see the series more as a cultural phenomenon that is simply a flash in the pan that will die out as soon as the seventh book appears telling the end of the story, if not before. They claim that young people read the books because of peer pressure and curiosity to see what all the fuss is about more than for any connection they may see or feel with the characters. Critics point to how the books are a "fast read," are badly edited (especially, they claim, book four), and seem to follow a formulaic pattern of a group of friends solving a mystery by piecing together clues dropped into the novels, with a climatic scene that always combines suspense, action, and adventure. They say that, like a television show, all of the action occurs within the same timeframe, in this case the length of a school year, and that the mystery gets solved before the characters return home for the summer.

Skeptics also point to the unprecedented amount paid in the American purchase of the rights to the books by Scholastic at auction. They say Rowling's rags-to-riches legend as a single parent trying to write fueled the hype and mystery surrounding her and her books, and that the hype continues as the movie adaptations pile onto the near-annual book releases. Critics also say that even the insatiable hunger created by popular culture in the early twenty-first century will be oversaturated with "Pottermania," and that the stories will lose their appeal once they are all in print and on film. When there is a lull between book publications as happened in 2002, skeptics argue, the enthusiasm of readers for the series wanes. They say the books will not stand up to time or in-depth analysis, but that the "Harry Potter Phenomenon" will be studied longer than the books themselves as a turn-of-the-millennium cultural moment.

Two things are certain when pondering which of these two views about the lasting qualities of J.K. Rowling's Harry Potter books is right. One is that not even the author, who is sharing the spotlight with Harry these days, knows which projection will come true. She has said that she will always write, that when all the Harry Potter books are done she will leave Hogwarts like her characters and start another project. In the meantime, her life appears to keep running along a parallel track with Harry's. While Harry is getting interested in relationships in books four and five, Rowling is enjoying a romance of her own. At Christmas 2001, she married a doctor she had met in Scotland one year before. The second thing that is sure about which prediction holds true—whether the Harry Potter books will be regarded as flashes in the pan or as timeless classics—is that only time, and the future, will tell. In the meantime, in her late thirties, Rowling's life proceeds full throttle. Before we try to catch up to the events in her life at the moment, it is important that we look back at where she's been and how she's gotten where she is.

Chapter 2

EARLY LIFE AND FAMILY

The woman behind the J. K. Rowling persona is, quite literally, a child of the 1960s. She was born in 1965, the middle year of one of the most turbulent decades of the twentieth century, a truly exciting time to be alive. That same summer the Beatles—who had "invaded" America the year before with a landmark appearance on the *Ed Sullivan Show* on CBS that would change rock and roll and popular culture forever—played Shea Stadium in Flushing, New York, to 60,000 screaming fans. It had been three years since the Americans put John Glenn into orbit, and landing the first man on the moon was still four years away. Seen in retrospect, it is fitting that UNICEF (United Nations International Children's Emergency Fund), one of Rowling's later interests, won the Nobel Peace Prize the same year that she was born.

Given that the success of this writer occurred at the turn of the century, it is interesting to consider the world into which J. K. Rowling was born. In the United States, Lyndon B. Johnson (Democrat from Texas) was president; in Great Britain, Harold Wilson (Lord Wilson of Rievaulx, Labor Party) was prime minister. It was the year Winston Churchill died and Malcolm X was assassinated. In 1965, the first American combat troops arrived in Vietnam, growing to 190,000 by December of that year. Popular movies released in 1965 included the classics *Dr. Zhivago* and *The Sound of Music*. The latter won the Oscar for best picture. The Watts riots occurred over six days in Los Angeles, and Martin Luther King, Jr. and 2,600 other civil rights activists were arrested in Selma, Alabama, for protesting voting registration rules. Poet T.S. Eliot died that year, as did singer Nat King Cole. Soviet cosmonaut Aleksei Leonov performed the first space walk.

During the *Gemini VIII* flight, American astronauts Wally Shirra and Tom Stafford performed the first docking of two spacecraft in space. The first commercial satellite, *Early Bird*, was launched. Rhodesia declared its independence from Great Britain. The Nobel Prize in Physiology and Medicine went to François Jacob, André Lwoff, and Jacques Monod (all French) for their study of regulatory activities in body cells.

In the world that would become Rowling's for a time at the turn of the century—the book world—publications the year she was born included Sylvia Plath's *Ariel* and *The Uncollected Poems*; Malcolm X's *Autobiography of Malcolm X*; Ralph Nader's *Unsafe at Any Speed*, an alert to consumers about the danger of the Ford Pinto; Eudora Welty's *Thirteen Stories*, and James Baldwin's *Going to Meet the Man*. The Newbery Medal went to *Shadow of a Bull* by Maia Wojciechowska, and the Carnegie Medal, Britain's counterpart award for best children's book, went to Philip Turner's *The Grange at High Force*. The Nobel Prize for Literature was awarded to a Soviet, Mikhail Sholokov.

In Britain during the week Jo Rowling was born, the Beatles' single "Help" was number one on the charts. Songs on the album and in the subsequent film include "Help," "Ticket to Ride," "Act Naturally," and "Yesterday." In many ways, Jo Rowling could probably adopt any one of these as her theme song for different periods in her life. If anyone ever wondered what effect Beatles music's driving beat and imagist lyrics may have had on a young child's life, certainly Jo Rowling's fertile imagination is one potential, natural outgrowth. She was born on July 31, in Cottage Hospital in Yate, the first child of Pete and Anne Rowling, married just four months before. They named her Joanne, and like her mother before her and her sister after her, Joanne was not given a middle name. Joanne's parents were just twenty years old when she was born.

In 1964, when they were still eighteen, Pete Rowling and Anne Volant were both serving their country. Pete had just joined the British Royal Navy, and Anne was a WREN (Women's Royal Naval Service). WRENs provided primarily clerical support to the navy. The two teenagers met on a train going from London's King's Cross station, 500 miles north to where they were stationed at 45 Commando, in Arbroath, Scotland. The long trip would prove to be the first of a series of train rides that would be important to J.K. Rowling. In addition, her parents' early life in Scotland foreshadowed her love affair with that country that continues today.

Pete and Anne hit it off at Kings Cross (Jo claims family folklore tells it was love at first sight), and they talked for hours and made arrangements to see each other again when they reached the base. Soon thereafter, however, the couple decided that the navy life was not for them, and they left military service. After seeing each other for several more months, the couple found themselves expecting a baby. They married on March 14, 1965, near Anne's parents' home at All Saints Parish Church in Tufnell Park, north of London. There was little they could do to conceal their predicament at the wedding. It was obvious that the couple's baby was already nearing the third trimester.

In the 1960s, the odds favoring a young married couple with a baby to support were no better than they are in the early twenty-first century. However, the Rowlings struggled and sacrificed to make a go of it. They moved into a simple, one-story house at 109 Sundridge Park in the town of Yate, some ten miles northeast of the city of Bristol. Pete got a job as an apprentice production engineer at the Bristol Siddeley aircraft engine factory while Anne stayed home preparing for the baby's arrival. Pete and Anne enjoyed being out of London, in a rural region of England called the West Country.

Historically, the West Country has had a romantic lure for Londoners who want to escape city life. It is more open, less crowded, with beautiful natural scenery and a long, often mysterious, history. Life is thought to be simpler there, less hectic, with an emphasis on having more time to enjoy other people and perhaps more opportunities to make a valued contribution to the community. Suburban sprawl, in the form of shopping malls and other developments, had not yet engulfed Yate as it has now, though it was even then considered to be a town without much character. Yate was not the perfect setting the Rowlings eventually wanted to live in, but it did give them a foothold in the West Country.

The different way of life the Rowlings sought by leaving the city was evident in the hospital where their baby was born. Cottage Hospital in Yate was formerly a private home called Melrose House, so it did not have the institutional look about it that many city and suburban hospitals have. Also, the building housed only a small maternity ward, making it a generally happy place to work in and be a patient. When young Anne checked in, she could count on a ten-day stay, which was a longer maternity stay than was regularly allowed in other hospitals, even at that time. She could also expect that she would come to know the other mothers who were there at the same time, since there would be less than a dozen of them in all, cared for under the guidance of Nellie—the hospital matron, Irene Norton.

The nearby town of Chipping Sodbury has a better ring to Jo Rowling's ear for names; she often tells people in interviews that she was born there. Ever the storyteller, perhaps Rowling believes the town's proximity to Yate makes it too good a name to pass up when she is asked about her birthplace. Chipping Sodbury is also a step up in economic class from Yate, which perhaps makes it more attractive to claim as a hometown. It is a quaint village with antique shops. The real estate is worth more money. Perhaps Rowling reveals class consciousness or perhaps she is just trying to protect her real birthplace from the mobs of tourists and visitors who would seek it out. For its part, Yate has a name and history that is interesting in its own right. The name is derived from the Saxon word *gete*, for "gate," meaning that the 2,000-year-old town was once a gateway to the woods of the royal hunting grounds. Gates to woods and mysterious places might be of interest to the adventurous mind of Jo Rowling, so perhaps she will reclaim Yate yet as her birthplace one day. In any case, the towns are so close to each other that it seems unlikely that people quibble much about Rowling's taking poetic license about her birthplace, especially when it is her storytelling ability that they most admire.

Whatever they thought of their first childbirth experience at the small Cottage Hospital, the Rowlings had their second child in an even smaller setting—at home at 109 Sundridge Park. Cottage Hospital did not allow child siblings of newborns in as visitors, so perhaps that was one reason behind the home birth. Jo states that the birth of her sister is her earliest memory. She recalls her father running in and out of the main bedroom where her mother had been in labor. She remembers her father giving her play dough that day to keep her busy. Reaching back to a memory that happened when she was not yet two years old, Jo does not recall seeing her new baby sister that day, but she does remember eating the play dough. Dianne Rowling was born on June 18, 1967, and Pete and Anne's family was complete. The Rowling girls, Joanne and Dianne, were very close in age and similar in name. Both girls' names contained the name of their mother, Anne. Likewise, both girls' names were shortened by those who knew them best to only two letters, and they became known to family and friends simply as Jo and Di.

Anne sometimes dressed the girls alike when they were quite young. In one childhood picture of them, both girls have round faces and trimmed bangs; they could almost be mistaken for twins by a quick passerby. Di was the more physically attractive of the two, according to Jo, who describes herself as a rather plain child. Jo says she was petite in stature, with bushy red hair, freckles, and later on, large, thick state-issued glasses—in other words, she says she was quite like the description of Hermione Granger in her Harry Potter books. Hermione is also described in the novels as having a slightly imperfect smile with two front teeth that protrude a bit. If this trait was shared by Jo as well, and if it bothered her to the point of self-consciousness, perhaps it might explain why so many photographs of her show her with a tight-lipped grin. Her full, wide white smile has only more recently appeared in publicity photos.

Not long after Di was born, the young Rowling family moved from Yate to 35 Nicholls Lane in Winterbourne, four miles away. Yate was beginning to expand in directions that only increased its lackluster character, and Pete Rowling found a neighborhood community on Nicholls Lane that was more like where he wanted to raise his family. Nicholls Lane had several three-bedroom stone houses, built only a few years before, into which other young families had moved.

Pete's income at the Bristol Siddeley factory was apparently sufficient that Anne could make the choice to stay home with their little girls while Pete stayed employed outside the home. A mother who enjoyed reading, Anne shared her love of books with her daughters, who flourished during the time she spent with them in their preschool years on Nicholls Lane. The house was filled with shelf upon shelf of books, so many that even several years later the neighbors remember the Rowlings as having a lot of books.

Pete added to the interest Anne was encouraging in the girls, providing Jo with her earliest memory of books. Jo remembers that when she was about four years old, she became sick with the measles, and her father read her Kenneth Grahame's *The Wind in the Willows*. She doesn't remember the illness, but she does remember the stories from that book. The book, a British children's literature classic originally published in 1908, contains a series of interconnected stories about the friendship of several animal characters: Mole, Rat, Mr. Toad, Badger, and their neighbors. There is a Wild Wood in the stories that is not unlike Rowling's own later creation, the Forbidden Forest. The animal characters in *The Wind in the Willows* quite possibly made an early impression on Jo's imagination that she would later call on when creating her own animal characters. Like Grahame, she also endowed the animal characters in her Harry Potter books with human characteristics, while at the same time not ignoring their inherent animal traits. Her attraction to animals also manifests itself in the creation of the giant gamekeeper, Hagrid, perhaps the most well known and beloved, and certainly the most soft-hearted when it comes to animals, gamekeeper in all of literature. Animals would continue to play a large part in Jo Rowling's life and work.

It was during these early years at 35 Nicholls Lane that Anne Rowling became friends with Ruby Potter, who lived at number 29. Ruby and her husband Graham had two children, Ian and Vikki, who were close in age to Jo and Di. Ruby stayed home to raise them as Anne was doing with her girls. The mothers would visit and swap books while their children jumped and romped across the yards with one another. Jo, the oldest of the four playmates, with an already lively imagination, was frequently the leader of their exploits.

One early indication of things to come was when Jo, Di, and the Potter kids used to swipe brooms from the garage and play witches and wizards, straddling them and zooming around the yard, pretending to fly on broomsticks. They would dress up for the part as well, often taking old clothing from their parents' dress-up boxes and transforming it into robes and other costumes. Ian Potter is said to remember borrowing an old long coat of his father's and a pair of joke glasses and running under a tree with the Rowling girls, where Jo would entertain them all with spells and stories—including all of them as characters. Ian remembers that Jo's made-up witches' brews, with ingredients as disgusting as possible, were of particular enjoyment to them.

When the first Harry Potter novel was published, Jo Rowling wrote to Ruby Potter that Harry is not a one-for-one depiction of her son, Ian. She has said that she used the Potter surname because she liked it and had fond memories of playing with the Potters as a young child. Observers might conjecture as well that these early, innocent, and protected days of playing in the neighborhood with friends provided Jo with fertile ground for her growing imagination and the security from which to explore new ideas. Certainly, going about most days in the company of a small group of friends was good practice for creating Harry Potter's own friendships many years later.

One of the playmates' misadventures could have provided an interesting stop on a Potterite tourist route had the situation not been corrected at the time. One day, Graham Potter, with the help of Ian's Uncle Roger, was adding a garage on to the Potter house. They had spread concrete for a cement floor, and it was still wet. Not unlike the adventures Harry Potter has in the novels, the "wizards" and "witches" of Nicholls Lane, led by Ian Potter, decided to step across the wet cement, imprinting their footprints like movie stars do in the sidewalk in front of Grauman's Chinese Theatre on Hollywood's Sunset Boulevard. When Mr. Potter expressed displeasure with this development, Pete Rowling came over to help, quite literally, smooth things over. One can only speculate what interest the tiny footprints of Jo Rowling, with Ian Potter's right alongside them, on the Potter's old garage floor would elicit today.

It is clear that friends have played an important role throughout Jo Rowling's life, and friendship is certainly a key relationship in the Harry Potter series. One reason for such reliance on friendship must certainly be that Jo's own family is very small. She has only one sister, whom she admits bossing around a lot as a child but with whom she is now very close. She vaguely remembers a cousin whom she hasn't seen for some years, and she has spoken about an aunt who read manuscripts for British publishers Mills and Boon and sent romantic novels to Anne that Jo would zip through very quickly. Since her parents were so young when she was born, Jo was lucky enough to get to know all four of her natural grandparents. She has admitted to using aspects of their personalities, both good and bad, in various characters in the Harry Potter books.

On her mother's side, Jo's grandparents are Stanley and Frieda Volant. Jo has described their marriage as an unhappy one. Jo remembers Frieda as having more affection for her many dogs than for little children. It is this trait that she imparts to Aunt Marge, the dog breeder who visits the Dursleys in *The Prisoner of Azkaban*. Aunt Marge makes several biting remarks to Harry that insult him, his mother, and especially the magical traits he inherited from her as opposed to the Muggle side of the family. If this scene dramatizes the emotional climate that existed between Frieda and her daughter, Anne, only Jo and her family know for sure. Sometimes mothers do not recover from disappointment in a daughter's premarital pregnancy; sometimes they do not approve of their daughters' choice in husbands or other choices they make in their lives. Perhaps there was discord between Jo's mother and her grandmother; perhaps not. In any case, Jo's response to the cruelty Aunt Marge shows to Harry is to have Harry blow her up and run away.

Jo admits to borrowing traits from her maternal grandfather, Stanley. He receives better treatment in *The Prisoner of Azkaban*. Stan Volant worked as a consultant engineer and later as a hospital mail carrier. He had such a dreamy imagination, according to Jo, that sometimes he confused fantasy with reality. He loved to tinker about the house, making things in his shed in Tufnell Park. Along with her grandfather Ernie, on her father's side, Jo memorializes not only traits of her grandfather Stan but also his name in *The Prisoner of Azkaban*. Stan and Ernie are the names of the Knight Bus drivers who rescue Harry Potter from the street.

Pete's parents, Ernie and Kathleen Rowling, ran a grocery store and lived in an apartment upstairs. The store was called Glenwood Stores, and it was situated on Station Road in West Moors, which is near Wimborne Minster in the area of England called Dorset. When there were no customers around when they came to visit, Ernie and Kathleen would let Jo and Di go downstairs and play store. As the older and self-described bossier sister, Jo got to be the shopkeeper, checking out the items that customer Di had gone around the store to purchase. Using real canned food, other items, and real money made their play particularly fun and special for them, and Jo remembers it fondly. They learned responsibility by putting everything back in its place when they were done playing. One wonders if this early play-shopping experience laid seeds for the future school shopping escapades on Diagon Alley that regularly appear in the Harry Potter books.

Jo's small "family" did extend to a few pets along the way. Her first pet was a dog named Thumper, after the comical rabbit friend of the deer Bambi in the 1962 Disney film. In *Bambi*, the fawn loses his mother to a hunter's gun. The young Bambi matures with the help of close friends from the forest, such as Thumper the rabbit and Flower the skunk. His father majestic, strong, and stately, with a full rack of sweeping antlers, appears out of the forest mist occasionally when Bambi is in greatest trouble. Loss of one's mother would prove to be an important theme later on in Jo Rowling's life and work. Bambi's father is reminiscent of the image Harry Potter sees of his father when he is confronting the dementors in *The Prisoner of Azkaban*. His father appears to Harry in the form of a stately stag, emerging from a misty white light and standing across from him on the other side of a lake. For his part, Thumper, the Rowling dog, became ill during Jo's childhood and was put to sleep, making Jo so sad that she still remembers how she felt.

Another set of pets the Rowling girls had were two guinea pigs. Unfortunately, they didn't last long. Both guinea pigs were left outside and got eaten by a fox. Jo recalls the unpleasantness of finding their bloody remains in the back yard. She had tropical fish as a teenager and still keeps fish as a hobby. The last pet Jo had at home was another dog, named Misty, which she had until she went to college.

One animal Jo probably never wanted as a pet was a tarantula or any other spiderlike creature. Ruby Potter remembers Jo's fear of spiders because her daughter, Vikki, is afraid of them, too. Jo created the scene in *Harry Potter and the Chamber of Secrets* in which Harry and his friend Ron Weasley confront Aragog and the other gigantic, hairy, nightmarish spiders that Hagrid has protectively hidden in the Forbidden Forest. She has admitted that the thing a Boggart would turn into in front of her (Boggarts turn into visions of what one most fears) would definitely be a giant spider.

Despite the animals they did have, Jo and Di always wanted a real rabbit as a pet. As inventive children do, when they can't have something in real life they often make believe they have it. Jo made up a story for Di where she falls down a rabbit hole, something like Alice does in *Alice's Adventures in Wonderland*, and is fed strawberries by the rabbit family she encounters there. An earlier story, the first one Jo remembers writing down when she was about five or six years old, was called "Rabbit." It was about a rabbit that got sick with the measles, and his friends who visited him, includii a pig and a fox. One of his friends was Miss Bee, a giant bee. Jo likely drew from her own experience in this very early story in which her character has the measles quite badly, like she had. Jo was already having fun naming her characters and creating friendships between them. She says that she went on to write a series of books about her Rabbit character, so possibly the notion of writing books in series began as early as that first attempt. Rowling claims that she stole most of her ideas for her first literary effort from a Richard Scarry story. That book could have been *I Am a Bunny*, published in 1967, when she was just two years old. The book features a bunny living with his friends in a forest through the different seasons of the year. This gentle story for very young children is still beloved by parents and families.

Writing her stories down was for Jo a natural outgrowth of hearing books read to her, reading them herself, and telling stories to her sister and friends in the neighborhood during their playtimes on the lane. The Rowlings did not watch much television, and fast food restaurants were sparse at that time and not a steady part of life in Winterbourne. Anne Rowling was a good cook, and she and Ruby Potter used to walk down to Sullivan's, the neighborhood grocery, and pick up fresh fruits and vegetables for dinner. There were no video games or computers in households during the sixties and early seventies, so Jo's imagination was free to develop and flourish on its own. Her steady diet of books, along with encouragement from her mother, fed her early efforts at storytelling.

While her mother read with her many of British writer Enid Blyton's Famous Five and Noddy books, Jo says now that she didn't care for them as much as she did books by Richard Scarry. Like many other girl readers, she went through her "horse phase" as well, perhaps a bit younger than some, since she had a picture book version of Anna Sewell's *Black Beauty* and other horse books. Black Beauty is a beautiful black mare that is treated cruelly and suffers much at the hands of several masters on a seemingly endless search for a home. Masters who appear to be friendly and kind toward Black Beauty at first turn out not to be what they seem over the course of their ownership. The cruelty shown toward the horse in this book is painful for many young readers. The theme of cruelty and people and things not being what they seem is one that comes up in Rowling's books, as well. One thinks of Malfoy's mistreatment of Buckbeak and its resultant beheading before time gets turned back to save him in *The Prisoner of Azkaban*. Hagrid's sadness and feelings of helplessness to do anything to protect his animal friend echo the reader's predicament in experiencing the novel *Black Beauty*.

Also like many other girl readers, Jo Rowling went through her *Little Women* phase, probably the most notable American title she mentions reading as a child. It would seem probable that she couldn't help noticing that she and Jo March shared more than just a name, and she admits that they shared identities in her imagination for at least a few months. Jo March is a strong female character who is the protagonist of *Little Women* by Louisa May Alcott. The second eldest of four sisters, Jo March is the leader of their playtimes together and perhaps exhibits the most imagination and certainly the most spunk of all four. In many ways, Jo March is the fictionalized Louisa May Alcott. Like Alcott, Jo March also wants to become a writer. Like Jo March, Jo Rowling would quickly develop the same secret desire.

Another aspect of *Little Women* that may have influenced Rowling is the emphasis and description of elaborate games from the girls' imaginations playacted in the attic, complete with costumes and scripts. Certainly these games must have brought to mind the same kinds of games Jo made up and played with her sister Di and the Potters on Nicholls Lane. Another important aspect of the book is its emphasis on the friendship that a neighbor boy, Laurie, develops with the Marches. The sisters befriend the lonely boy who lives with his grandfather, Mr. Laurence. Like the Harry Potter books, *Little Women* also follows the characters through adolescence, and the reader sees changes in the relationships and priorities of the characters as they mature.

The book Jo mentions most frequently and with greatest fondness from her early reading is the 1946 British children's fantasy, Elizabeth Goudge's *The Little White Horse*, little known in the United States. Jo claims that this book, above all others, most directly influenced the first Harry Potter book especially. The similarities are certainly there for readers who might be interested to seek them out. The book won a Carnegie Medal in England in 1946 and was produced many years later by the BBC with the title *Moonacre*. The novel's protagonist, Maria Merryweather, is a plain, red-haired girl with much spirit, a character akin to Jo Rowling's description of herself as a girl and not unlike Hermione from her Harry Potter books. Like Harry Potter, Maria Merryweather is an orphan. Also, like Harry, Maria is an orphan who is rescued from a dull, drab life to find out that she has a special role in a fantastic world she previously knew nothing about. Maria is taken to the West Country, the general area where Rowling grew up, and is led through a door in a rock that leads through a tunnel to a magical, silvery kingdom. There she is led to a castle where she discovers that she is the princess of Moonacre Valley, and everyone there already knows who she is. Readers of *Harry Potter* will recognize the similarity of Maria to Harry, since Harry is led through a brick wall to Diagon Alley and on to Hogwarts (presumed to be in Scotland) aboard the Hogwarts Express. He discovers that he is a wizard, a famous one, whom everyone there already knows.

Rowling shares Goudge's appreciation for finding or making up unusual names. In *The Little White Horse,* there is a Miss Heliotrope (Maria's governess), a Monsieur Cocq de Noir, Loveday Minette, and even a small elf like Dobby, named Marmaduke Scarlet.

Playing off both the realistic and the fantastic, Goudge gives special powers to the animals in her book. It takes a bit of time before the reader comes to the delightful realization that Wiggins, for example, is a dog and not a human. Another dog, Wrolf, turns out to be a lion that protects Maria, and a cat, Zachariah, has the special ability of writing hieroglyphics in the hearth ashes with its tail. These traits remind Rowling's readers of animal characters like Scabbers, who is really Pettigrew in Animagus form, and Hermione's cat, Crookshanks, who can see this other identity in Scabbers and tries to protect Hermione and her friends from Pettigrew. The little white horse in Goudge's novel turns out to be a unicorn. Unicorns appear in Rowling's Forbidden Forest, as well, where their blood is a silvery, mercurylike fluid that has been mysteriously spilled on the ground. The villain, Voldemort, drinks it to stay alive.

Writers of both novels appear to like to write about feasts, describing the food in detail, like a camera shot panning slowly down a long banquet table. It's amusing to think of growing children, who are always hungry, feasting their eyes and imaginations on the descriptions of food in these books. Jo has said she recalls Goudge's descriptions as so intricate that they even tell what ingredients are in the sandwiches. Of course, both writers knew that food combines the sensory details of the visual with taste and smell, which makes their fantastic worlds come alive in an intimate way for all their readers, regardless of age.

Fighting evil with courage and friendship is another attribute of the novel that Jo used when she wrote *Harry Potter.* She has said she loved the plot of *The Little White Horse,* which moved right along and included romance with fearsome adventure and a strong female protagonist.

The novel is one of the few about which Jo speaks of the quality of its writing and the way it is put together. She admires the way the story is built and says it stands up under rereadings, since readers seem to accumulate layers of meaning and understanding with each read. With her high endorsement, the novel has recently enjoyed fresh reprintings that have made it more available in the United States.

By 1974, when Jo was nine years old and had already attended school in Winterbourne for a few years, life would change dramatically for her and the rest of the Rowling family. Things were very different in the world by then, as well. In 1974, foiled by the Watergate scandal and served with three articles of impeachment by the United States House of Representatives, Richard Nixon became the first United States president to resign from office. Vice President Gerald Ford became the new president and pardoned his old boss as one of his first acts in office. The excitement over the first man walking on the moon five years earlier was already fading, as was monetary support for other lunar missions. That year Patricia Hearst, daughter of the publishing executive Randolph Hearst, was kidnapped by the Symbionese Liberation Army. India tested a nuclear device successfully, making it the sixth world nuclear power. A leftist revolution ended almost fifty years of dictatorial rule in Portugal, a country that would be important later on in Rowling's life. In Ethiopia, Emperor Haile Selassie was deposed, bringing in a military dictatorship to that country.

Deaths of well-known people in 1974 included Charles Lindbergh and Duke Ellington. Ed Sullivan, who had brought the Beatles to the attention of American fans on his show the year Jo Rowling was born, also died that year. In sports, West Germany defeated Holland 2–1 in the World Cup. Chris Evert and Jimmy Connors won the women's and men's finals at Wimbledon, and the Oakland As beat the Dodgers in the World Series. Cannonade won the Kentucky Derby.

That year the Nobel Peace Prize went to Sean MacBride of Ireland and Eisaku Sato of Japan for their work toward peace in their respective countries and internationally. The Nobel Prize for Literature was shared by two Swedish writers, Eyvind Johnson and Harry Martinson, and the Nobel Prize for Physics that year went to Martin Ryle and Antony Hewish of the United Kingdom, for their discovery of pulsars.

While Jo Rowling experimented at home with pencil and paper and a dreamy imagination, books published in 1974 included Toni Morrison's *Sula*, Stephen King's *Carrie*, Gary Snyder's *Turtle Island*, and Annie Dillard's *Pilgrim at Tinker Creek*. In children's literature, the Newbery Medal went to *The Slave Dancer* by Paula Fox, and *The Stronghold* by Molly Hunter won the Carnegie. Popular culture maintained its movement of merging personalities from different media together, evidenced by *People* magazine's debut in 1974, with Mia Farrow on the cover.

In music, Patti Smith released "Hey, Joe," a song thought to be the first punk rock single. The Beatles had broken up four years earlier, in 1970, but three of the fab four released solo albums in 1974: John Lennon's *Walls and Bridges*; George Harrison's *Dark Horse*; and Ringo Starr's *Goodnight*

Vienna. Paul McCartney had released *Band on the Run* the year before. The mid-seventies seemed like an aftershock to the tumult of the preceding decade.

In 1974, Anne and Pete Rowling found a house even closer to the country living they had always imagined when they left London behind and moved to the West Country. In their drives over the newly opened Severn Bridge across the Severn River to enjoy the countryside in the Forest of Dean near Wales, they had spotted an old stone cottage that was up for sale. When they inquired and found out that the price was right for Church Cottage, which was nestled next door to St. Luke's Church, plans for moving to the more pastoral and scenic area were set in motion. After they discovered that Tutshill School of England, which their two girls could attend, was on the other side of St. Luke's, the move became inevitable.

Anne and Pete put their Nicholls Lane house in Winterbourne up for sale. Since couples and young families are always looking for three-bedroom houses in kindly neighborhoods like Nicholls Lane in which to start and raise their families, the For Sale in the front yard quickly caught the attention of Tanya and Dave Cowles. Anne was vacuuming when the Cowles stopped by to take a look, and she proudly showed Tanya her garden, where she had planted, among other things, a staghorn fern and a pink weigela. Anne gave Tanya a potted plant of white violets. The Cowles were sold on the house; they offered $16,500, which Pete readily accepted, since he was eager to move to Church Cottage.

If Jo's early childhood experiences in Winterbourne provided a foundation for her love of books, animals, and friends, surely her new surroundings provided her with exposure to the wonder of magical places. The community of Tutshill was small and middle class, nestled between two rivers, the Severn and the Wye, and bordering the Forest of Dean. The Forest of Dean covers 203 square miles between these two rivers in the southwest of England on the northern side of the Bristol Channel.

The southern area of the forest is quite different from the northern portion. The North is characterized by rich rolling lands, landscaped gardens, and timbered houses dating back to the seventeenth century. The South, which is the area bordered by Tutshill, encompasses 27,000 acres of ancient forest that date back to the times before the Romans. Old Roman roads still exist and are visible in the area; still more wait to be excavated. The forest was used during the Dark Ages, as a hunting ground during the Norman period, as well as a resource for timber for fighting ships. While the forest retains much of its natural beauty—with various conifer, oak, and beech trees—other of the forest's resources have been pillaged over the years. The forest has known miners of coal, iron, and stone, in addition to its timber harvesting

Visitors to the Forest of Dean today can take themed tours of old churches and old villages that predate those in the United States by hundreds of years. Other visitors might take a flora and fauna tour, much like one would at a National Park in the United States, or they might decide to take a literary tour. Several authors in England came from the Forest of Dean area. These include: Dennis Potter (a name not lost on Harry Potterites), Winifred Foley, F. W. Harvey, and the Dymock Poets. Several years after she moved to the area as a young girl, J. K. Rowling would be added to this list.

The deep, ancient history of the forest gave rise to stories and myths that made it a magical place to explore. Jo talks about wandering along the river Wye and the open fields alone with her sister Di. Tutshill lies on the border of England and Wales. The nearest Welsh town, Chepstow, is only a mile downhill from Tutshill. Though Tutshill resides in the English county of Gloucestershire, it is, in many ways, indistinguishable from a Welsh town.

The River Wye has a rich history in its own right. People from the gentry class, born to wealth and privilege, used to make a grand tour of the countryside along the Wye to view the beautiful scenery on a pleasant day. In the eighteenth century, the Wye was a major shipping route of goods from Chepstow to Hereford in the interior of Wales. Today the river and its valley provide a source of outdoor activities from canoeing to kayaking, from rock climbing to exploring caves, to walking along its shores on a path that is more than fifty miles long. Four years before the Rowlings moved there, the Wye Valley, which makes up the western border of the Forest of Dean area, was designated an Area of Outstanding Natural Beauty. The forest is also called the Royal Forest of Dean, not inappropriately, since Prince Charles, the Duke of Wales, lives not far away and visits its natural splendor frequently with Prince William and Prince Harry.

Other landmarks and features of the area make it fascinating for readers of the Harry Potter series to imagine the author growing up there. One is Tutshill Tower, which sits on an overlook in Tutshill and looks like a remnant from an old castle. It is thought to be a beacon or lighthouse dating from the sixteenth century. Still another is the formidable eleventh-century castle overlooking the River Wye in Chepstow, the village next to Tutshill. Chepstow Castle is a Norman castle with a long history; its key vantage point on the cliff overlooking the river must have been enough to set any imaginative mind, much less the fertile mind of the future creator of Harry Potter and Hogwarts, wondering about stories and adventures that occurred there.

Still another interesting treasure found in this area is world-famous Tintern Abby, which British poet William Wordsworth made famous in his poem, "Lines Composed a Few Miles Above Tintern Abbey, on Revisting the Banks of the Wye during a Tour, July 13, 1798." The poem begins:

> FIVE years have past; five summers, with the length
> Of five long winters! and again I hear
> These waters, rolling from their mountain-springs
> With a soft inland murmur.—Once again
> Do I behold these steep and lofty cliffs,
> That on a wild secluded scene impress
> Thoughts of more deep seclusion; and connect
> The landscape with the quiet of the sky.

The ruins of Tintern Abby (or Abaty Tyntyrn in Welsh) are located down the River Wye, a short distance from Chepstow. It is the most well preserved abby in all of Wales and was built by the Cistercians in the year 1131. It was rebuilt in the thirteenth and fifteenth centuries and became the largest abby in the country. At present, it stands open to the elements; its roof and windows are missing, and its floors are covered with a carpet of green grass. It's hard to know whether Jo Rowling was inspired in any way by Tintern Abby or by the Wordsworthian poem that it inspired. She has said that she has not been in the habit of reading poetry. However, certainly the presence of the abby and the countryside the poem depicts were part of the history and landscape that contributed to the atmosphere of the new community in which Jo Rowling and her family found themselves in 1974.

As if the amazing old buildings weren't enough to set the imagination in motion, another relevant feature of the Wye Valley is its wildlife. The year-round presence of peregrine falcons along the river attracts birders, scientists, and other naturalists. The peregrine falcon is a fast hunter, zooming down toward its prey in a powerful, high-speed dive, not unlike seeker Harry Potter diving on his broomstick to catch a Quidditch golden snitch.

Other birds in the region include those that stay close to the rivers, lakes, and streams and have names that might have been tempting to name-gathering Jo Rowling: coot, heron, grey wagtail, reed warbler, mute swans, and welducks. Garden birds and countryside birds of Wales, which

Rowling might have seen flitting about her backyard or in the fields and forest nearby, include owls of various kinds, such as barn owl, tawny owl, and short-eared owl; various types of finches, including bullfinches and chaffinches; ravens and snipes and buzzards; jays and magpies and a variety called the willow warbler. There are fewer reptiles in Wales and other parts of Great Britain than elsewhere in the world. Those in Wales include the common lizard, grass snake, adder, and slow worm.

The clean water of the Wye, its low-lying wetlands, and its wildlife helped the area earn the designation as a Site of Special Scientific Interest (SSSI). Amphibians native to Wales include frogs and toads, newts and crayfish. Mammals include rabbits, red squirrels, the dormouse, moles, hedgehogs, badger, fox, bats, mink, polecats, brown rats, and another small, furry animal called a shrew. Insects include dragonflies, butterflies, and beetles, among others.

The plants and flowers of the Forest of Dean contribute to the magical nature of the place. Along with the many commonly known plants like violets, bluebells, and daffodils are those with interesting names such as germander speedwell and ivyleaved toadflax. Fungi in the forest and the surrounding area include names that would delight any Potterite: dead man's fingers, yellow brain fungus, dung roundhead, scarlet elfcup, stinkhorn, parrot wax cap, amethyst deceiver, the blusher, brain purple-drop, penny bun, slippery Jack, fairy parasol, Dryad's saddle, and horsehair fungus. These are just a few!

Church Cottage and the surrounding area provided just the sort of life Anne and Pete Rowling had been hoping for when they moved away from London as a young couple and sought out the West Country. Pete had wanted to find an old house and restore it and modify it, keeping the charm of its antiquity but adding some of the comforts of modern living. Church Cottage served as the first school building for St. Luke's Church in 1848. It had flagstone floors and an ancient covered well underneath the living room. When their old friends from Nicholls Lane visited for a housewarming party, Pete showed them these features of the cottage, but guests also noticed that Pete had installed one of the first gas fireplaces that they had ever seen in a private home.

While the move was a dream come true for Pete and Anne, it was anything but dreamlike for their daughters, Jo and Di, then nine and seven. The move meant leaving Nicholls Lane and their friends the Potters behind. It meant going to a new school and making new friends. Most of all, it meant getting used to the peculiar way of life in Tutshill, a tiny community that prided itself on staying outside the mainstream by clinging to many of the old ways of doing things.

For an intelligent, imaginative girl on the verge of adolescence in the mid-1970s, who had left behind a new house in a neighborhood of new houses in a bigger town on the outskirts of Bristol, this move to an older, smaller community marked a definite shift in what had been, until then, a peaceful and happy childhood.

Chapter 3

THE SCHOOL YEARS

Education has played an especially important role in the life of J. K. Rowling. Rowling attended five different British institutions of learning during her own formal education and taught or student taught in at least four others in France, Portugal, and Scotland. Her mother came from a family of teachers, and Jo became certified to teach modern languages in Scotland the year before the first Harry Potter book was published by Bloomsbury in England.

Rowling's creation, the castlelike Hogwarts School of Witchcraft and Wizardry, is probably the best-known fictional institution of learning in the world today. Hogwarts is the primary setting for the Harry Potter books, and the principal characters are, with few exceptions, either students, teachers, staff, or ghosts and poltergeists who populate the school. Characters who are not at Hogwarts tend to be either alumni or former or current guests from other wizardry schools. There is life outside school grounds in the Harry Potter novels, but so far in the series all roads or passageways leading away from Hogwarts School of Witchcraft and Wizardry eventually lead back to the school in one way or another.

In today's reading world, the Harry Potter books rarely sit idle on school library shelves; they are assigned as class projects and are even assigned as reading in college courses. With education such a focal point in the Harry Potter novels, it is interesting, and perhaps important to the reading of the novels themselves, to take a closer look at the formal educational journey of Jo Rowling herself.

PRIMARY SCHOOL

In September 1970, Anne Rowling walked five-year-old daughter Jo to her first day of school at St. Michael's Church of England School on High Street in Winterbourne. It was only a five-minute walk from their home at 35 Nicholls Lane. Jo would go to the infant school section of St. Michael's for two years before transferring over to the junior school.

On that first day, so important to parents and children alike, Jo wore the school uniform, which consisted of a gray skirt and red top. The special walk must have been filled with the usual first-day excitement. St. Michael's has a cozy architecture, with bay windows on a building that looks a bit like a Victorian chapel. It had an open-plan classroom arrangement and was a comfortable place for young children to be. Jo liked it very much.

The most vivid memory Jo has of her first day of school, however, was when Anne came at lunchtime to pick her up. She thought that when the first day at school was over, that was that; there would be no more school. Apparently, as the first child in the family to go out to school, it had not yet sunk in to this future teacher that this would be her daily routine for many years. After the customary first two years in infant school when she was five and six years old, Jo at age seven moved to St. Michael's junior school, which, though at a slightly different location on Linden Close, was still just a five-minute walk from home, only in the opposite direction.

In the fall of 1972, the principal, or headmaster, of St. Michael's junior school was Alfred Dunn, whose initials and occupation have caused some to wonder how close he might be to being one of the real-life models for Albus Dumbledore, the headmaster at Hogwarts School of Witchcraft and Wizardry. Dunn does not remember young Jo. She was one of the quieter students and, with a July birthday, she was also one of the youngest in her class all the way through school. Dunn is now in his eighties and appears to have enjoyed the attention that Harry Potterites and the media have given him, even if other connections to the famous Hogwarts headmaster are rather thin and Jo has never suggested any deference to him.

While the teachers and staff claim that the studies have changed considerably in thirty years, with children being expected to grow up much faster nowadays, there are still some elements at St. Michael's that are the same as when Jo attended as a young child. They still have a tradition, for example, of celebrating May Day with a maypole in the playground, and the school marks the feast day of St. Michael every September 29 with an event they call the Michaelmas Mop Fair. The same old bell that Jo would have heard, marked A.R.P. for Air Raid Patrol from the days of the world wars long before her time, chimes to bring the children back into the classroom from recess.

Ruby Potter's children attended the same school as Jo and Di, and Ruby and Anne would often wait together for their children to be dismissed from school in the afternoon. Frequently, they would go to the park or on some other short outing to help the children let off steam before they went back home to begin preparing the evening meal and getting the children started on their homework.

School must have set a predominantly positive tone for Jo, who had enjoyed books even before she arrived. The early, sheltered years at St. Michael's provided her with a good foundation for considering school as a positive experience. She would need that foundation when she faced a very different classroom in the fall of 1974.

When they moved into Church Cottage, the Rowlings left behind their seemingly idyllic life in Winterbourne. Jo and Di needed to get used to the new village of Tutshill, an old-fashioned town that was very different from the more modern Winterbourne. They also had to get used to a new house, which was an old, nineteenth century schoolhouse in its own right, and a new school almost next door that was altogether different from their earlier school.

The old stone Church Cottage sat beside St. Luke's Church and a graveyard. Jo would say many years later that she enjoyed living beside the graveyard, even though her friends thought it was creepy. She says that graveyards are a great place to collect names. On the other side of St. Luke's was Tutshill Church of England Primary School, which Jo and Di would attend. The stone building was used for both school and church services from 1848 until St. Luke's was consecrated in 1853. Until 1893, the cottage remained the main school building. In the United States, the word "cottage" denotes a small, cozy house, but Church Cottage was not small. The Rowlings had moved into an old schoolhouse that once had provided classroom space for nearly 100 students at a time, as well as church services for a congregation of 120. When it was fixed up, the house represented a move up for the Rowlings in terms of their living quarters, both in size and prestige.

The history of the cottage in its school days might be interesting to today's students. The Education Act of 1880 made school mandatory for children up to the age of ten. After age ten, children could leave school if they had shown adequate attendance up until that time. If they lacked the required number of attendances, they had to keep coming to school until the age of thirteen. Students often did not go to school, even before the age of ten. School records at Tutshill indicate that the reasons for absences back in the 1800s were principally illness and the weather, but children also missed school because they had to help with farm work, such as haying, planting potatoes, taking wool to the market, or picking apples.

One interesting anecdote centers around a day off at the school, when the children received a holiday on May 12, 1885, to attend the wedding of their needlework teacher. Miss Maggie Evans processed into St. Luke's Church over a path of flowers laid there for her by her students.

As romantic as this history may sound today, the rules had changed dramatically for students nearly 100 years later when Jo Rowling started school at Tutshill, in the building the school had moved into when it left Church Cottage. Jo has described Tutshill Church of England Primary School as something straight out of a Charles Dickens novel. If the comparison is accurate, this implies strict codes of conduct, high expectations, and teachers who themselves seem barely able to tolerate life on any given day, much less lead a roomful of children in interesting exercises to help improve their skills in reading, writing, and arithmetic. One such teacher was Mrs. Sylvia Morgan, the first instructor Jo encountered in her new school in her new town and one whom she has discussed openly.

Jo arrived in class in uniform that first day after walking the few steps from the door of Church Cottage. Tutshill's uniform consisted of an Oxford blue sweater and skirt with a Cambridge blue blouse. She slid into a desk that was again something out of a Dickens novel, with its wooden rolltop complete with inkwell lined up straight with those in front and back of it in defined, orderly rows. The other students were probably not much less fearful than Jo was that first day of school in Year 9. Mrs. Morgan had a reputation around school that terrorized the students who had not been in her class. Out of fear, the children in the room were probably particularly quiet that first day as somewhere between thirty-five and forty students sat at their desks and surveyed Mrs. Morgan while considering their chances for survival until June.

Mrs. Morgan, a short stout woman with an annoying, frequent sigh and what seemed to the students a permanent expression of disapproval, evidently had her methods for surveying her new students as well. She gave them a math test the first thing that morning and from the scores decided who was bright and who was not, assigning the students their seats accordingly. Jo remembers this "Daily Ten" mental math test and how miserably she fared that first day. She scored only half a point on the test, primarily because the test involved fractions, which she had not been taught at St. Michael's. Mrs. Morgan promptly moved her to what Jo has called the "dim row," which was on the right hand side of the room.

Jo made friends in Mrs. Morgan's classroom, which is an important achievement to any new student in a new town. However, as she improved in her math skills and was moved to the "bright" side of the room at the left (apparently, one was not doomed to stay either "dim" or "bright" the entire year in Mrs. Morgan's estimation), these attachments loosened, and Jo was left again feeling out of place and needing to start over in the hard work of developing friendships. So, while she had taken on Mrs. Morgan's challenge to improve in math and won, she did so at the cost of her own comfort with her peers. Jo has acknowledged her own likeness at age eleven to Hermione Granger from the Harry Potter novels. Observers might see this tough choice of academics over friendships in Mrs. Morgan's class as foreshadowing the same character trait in the Hermione-like girl Jo would become less than two years later.

In her Harry Potter novels, Jo has admitted modeling Professor Snape on a few of her most memorable and least favorite people from her past, and she has said that Mrs. Morgan from Year 9 at Tutshill Primary was definitely one of them. Readers can look to the fear Mrs. Morgan engendered in her students as a prime source of the power that fuels Jo's expression of this fright so many years later as Harry, Hermione, and Ron contend with Professor Snape.

Mrs. Morgan wasn't the only problem for the students at Tutshill; they also had to face the unpleasant prospect of having her husband, John Morgan, who was also deputy headmaster, the very next fall in Year 10. John's teaching style, however, proved to be much different from his wife's, and the students soon learned that they needn't fear he would try to outdo his wife in strictness. In fairness to the Morgans, they were both involved and well liked in the community.

Anne and Pete Rowling did not abandon their daughters when they moved them into the old schoolhouse in the strange, old-fashioned town of Tutshill. The following year they signed Jo and Di up for outside activities such as Brownies. Perhaps typical of children's organizations in the Forest of Dean area, the Brownie packs had rather magical names such as "Elves," "Pixies," "Fairies," and "Gnomes." Among their community service projects in 1975, the year Jo joined, was helping the elderly of their area with various odd jobs, and they won an award from the Forest of Dean Round Table for their efforts.

At the same time, Jo and Di were learning much about the wonderful scenery along the River Wye and the mystical place that was the Forest of Dean. Jo has spoken of herself and Di enjoying their times exploring the spots around the boulders at Offa's Dyke on the River of Wye. As they got older, they would walk along the pathway on the river and imagine stories and adventures at Chepstow Castle, which sat high up on the cliff overlooking the river.

Jo maintained her thirst for reading during this period as well, picking up books by such authors as Edith Nesbit, Enid Blyton, and series such as *What Katy Did* by Susan Coolidge and C. S. Lewis's well-known *Chronicles of Narnia*. Jo also has said that she read romances and spy novels sent to the house by her great aunt, who was a reader for Mills and Boon publishers. She remembers reading her first James Bond novel, Ian Fleming's *Thunderball*, at age nine and being totally taken away by the notion that there could be a drink called a "bloody Mary."

Another event that marked the early years in Tutshill for Jo in a less than pleasant way was her first memory of the death of a relative. When she was nine, Jo's grandmother, Kathleen Rowling, died of a heart attack. This was Stanley's wife, who, along with her husband, had let Jo and Di play store in the market they owned beneath their apartment. With all the problems Jo had in school and fitting in at Tutshill, she says that losing her Grandmother Kathleen is still her saddest memory of that time. She would later give her grandmother a lasting tribute when she adopted the middle initial K. for Kathleen in her pen name.

The Morgans are now both dead, and Tutshill Church of England Primary School has changed its interior in an effort to make it more cheerful and welcoming to today's students. While it still values its traditions, there is a move toward encouraging a philanthropic attitude in its students toward some of its famous former student's pet organizations such as Comic Relief. However, Tutshill School had left a permanent mark on the young girl who had to live right next door to the school building both day and night and who spent the first year in her new surroundings in fear. Though she would live at her parents' beloved Church Cottage for many more years, through secondary school, and though she has been invited back for different events, including the 150th anniversary of Tutshill School in 1998, Jo only recently returned to Tutshill, and that was to take a look at the outside of Church Cottage for a television interview in late 2001. Tutshill's influence on the Harry Potter series appears to be more implicit in the characters' personalities and in the appearance of settings than it is explicit. In any case, the only mention of the town thus far in Rowling's books is very brief, and that is as a team in *Quidditch Through the Ages*.

SECONDARY SCHOOL

Most of the students who went to Tutshill went the two miles down the road to Sedbury to enroll in Wyedean Comprehensive Secondary School. That is what Jo Rowling did in the fall of 1976. To American students unfamiliar with the British system, it is perhaps easiest to think of the seven years at comprehensive secondary school in Britain as the seven years, or books, of the *Harry Potter* series, which are equivalent to Grades 6–12 in the United States. Like Harry, Jo was eleven years old when she began at Wyedean, and since they share July 31 birthdays, Jo was seventeen years old when she graduated, as Harry will be if he graduates from Hogwarts.

Just like Hermione Granger, Jo Rowling entered Wyedean at age 11, wearing her brown and yellow uniform and ready to make an impression with her intelligence and her good grades. She says that her hand was the first to go in the air, and she became known around the school for snobbishness, although this attitude probably masked shyness and insecurity more than anything else. Wyedean was a state school that drew students from a diverse population. Students from long-standing rural families mixed with those from families who had moved to the West Country from London and brought with them more money and different ideas. By her early teens, Jo had moved away a bit from her desire for academic superiority and made more friends. Perhaps a look at her reading at the time tells the difference. She says that when she was eleven or twelve she read Jane Austen's *Pride and Prejudice*. By fourteen, she was reading Jessica Mitford's *Hons and Rebels*.

Jo still claims Jane Austen is her favorite writer of all time. Austen's *Pride and Prejudice*, published in 1813, concerns the feisty Elizabeth Bennet and several matchmaking adventures and misadventures among the young adult characters of Fitzwilliam Darcy, George Wickham, Charles Bingley, Charlotte Lucas, and Elizabeth and Jane Bennet. The novel is full of wit, characteristic of Austen, and plenty of commentary on what Austen saw as the petty social practices of the well-off classes of her day. Elizabeth Bennet was said to have been Austen's favorite character in her books.

In *Emma*, which Jo has read several times and says is her favorite novel, Austen returns to her sharp and telling wit, after straying from it a bit in another novel, *Mansfield Park*. *Emma*, published in 1816, is about Emma Woodhouse, a pretty, clever, and independent young woman who likes to do a bit of matchmaking and meddling in Harriet Smith's advancement in life. When her efforts go awry, she risks extreme embarrassment but comes to self-knowledge that is very valuable. As another chess-game sort of plot

involving three or four country village families, this novel is often regarded as one of Austen's great masterpieces. Emma progresses from being
a deluded young woman to knowing herself through events that do not go
at all as she planned because of several errors in judgment. As an independent woman herself, perhaps Jo Rowling can identify to some degree
with Emma Woodhouse, coming to self-knowledge and seeing reality up
close because of several errors in judgment she made later on in her adult
life.

Jo's great aunt gave her *Hons and Rebels* by Jessica Mitford when she
was fourteen. The book is a memoir about Mitford's rambunctious and
mischievous childhood with her sisters and her eventual elopement with
Esmond Romilly, nephew of Winston Churchill, as well as her political
and military involvement with the Spanish Civil War. Ironically, in *Hons
and Rebels*, Mitford describes reading a book herself at age fourteen that
inspired her political leanings. The book was *Cry Havoc* by Beverley
Nichols, which is about the first World War and advocates disarmament.
Jo has said that she admires Mitford's idealism and courage, traits she most
respects in individuals, particularly strong women. Mitford's autobiography stands out from the list of titles Jo is known to have read as a youth,
which were mostly classic novels, fantasies, and the romance and spy novels that her aunt kept sending to Jo's mother, Anne. Jo admits that *Hons
and* Rebels made a lasting impression on her, so much so that she later
named her daughter after its author.

Mitford came from a wealthy, well-connected English family. Like Jane
Austen, she had a rebellious nature that found many of the structures and
expectations of her class and times trivial, boring, or downright funny.
Hons and Rebels is her account of growing up and seeing past what was expected of her to embrace ideals she set for herself. It is written in the first
person, and Mitford's engaging voice makes her memoir read much like a
well-plotted fictional story. It has adventure, danger, luck, and tragedy.

Jo has said that one of the episodes she admires most is how Jessica
Mitford ran away from home and had the gall to charge a camera on her
father's credit card without his knowledge or approval. Jo says she'd
never have had the nerve to do such a thing, but she admired Jessica because she did. Women who defy strong fathers and family ties to seek out
their dreams and follow their convictions often inspire other women who
are too timid to do the same. Later, when Jo wanted to major in one area
in college, she yielded to her parents' wishes and majored in another, related field because her parents thought it more practical. This is an indication that Jo wanted to please her parents, or at least not trouble them.
Mitford, on the other hand, could probably be seen as more courageous,

since following her political causes set her on a dangerous path, risking her family's blessing. In a family as flamboyant and diverse as the Mitfords, however, the risk of being separated from the family was probably not as great as it may have appeared to be to the fourteen-year-old Jo Rowling.

Back in secondary school at Wyedean, where she continued to earn good grades, aspects of Jo's family life were changing. This included her mother's employment status. The chemistry teacher at the time, John Nettleship, whose wife, Shirley, was the head lab technician, needed another lab technician for the school. With Di also enrolled at Wyedean, Anne Rowling applied for the job. When Anne was called in for the position, she took the job at once.

Anne was very well liked by the staff and students around the school. She helped out with the Tutshill Youth Club evenings after school and played the guitar pretty well, which she taught Jo to play. Soon, the secondary school community came to know Jo, Di, and Anne coming into and out of the school buildings in the mornings and afternoons together, almost like three sisters.

For Jo, however, John Nettleship's chemistry class was no easy task. He liked to pick on students out of the blue to answer questions, often frightening them even though they came to class prepared. Jo struggled in chemistry, but Nettleship picked on her anyway, which he says he did because she was one of the brightest in the class. The uneasiness of Harry Potter's relationship to Professor Snape has often been traced back to John Nettleship by those who know Jo's former teachers. While striking fear in his students, he showed an odd sense of respect for them at the same time, and there was a hint of puzzlement on the part of the students over whether or not what he did was for their own good. While how much Nettleship influenced the character of Professor Snape is unknown, the connection between Nettleship's chemistry class and chemistry and potions in the Harry Potter books is clearer.

The class Jo says she liked least at Wyedean was what Americans would call "shop." This class included metalworking and woodworking, and Jo says that she was terrible at both. Preferring to dream up stories rather than work with her hands, Jo could never quite catch on to just why one did things like hammer metal or know quite when to stop once she started hammering. She says her mother kept a teaspoon she made that had no cupped portion at all—it was completely flat and useless. She also remembers bringing home a picture frame that had more glue on it than wood. Although she didn't necessarily mind gym class, especially swimming and dancing, she was no star athlete and disliked hockey intensely.

Luckily for Jo, Wyedean's English teachers were beginning to notice and praise her creative efforts at writing. Jo was less inclined to speak out in class than she was to put her ideas and observations about a given question on paper, and her new teachers were able to see that. In addition, the English classes themselves were growing more sophisticated and varied, both in terms of the reading material and the openness to different kinds of writing, like imaginative writing.

By far, Jo's favorite teacher at Wyedean was an English teacher named Lucy Shepherd. A young teacher in her twenties, Lucy already had an edge in gaining the attention of many of her teenaged students, since she wasn't that much older than they were. She also had fresh ideas, such as encouraging the young women in her classes to speak out and to work towards attaining a career in a field they liked and had a talent for, without necessarily putting family plans in front of those desires. This was the middle and late 1970s, when the women's movement was enjoying a second wave of impassioned champions, and Lucy Shepherd was one of them.

Lucy did not necessarily teach with a soft touch, however. Jo describes her as strict and even abrasive at times with her students. Jo respected her for being conscientious with them; she really believed that Miss Shepherd cared that they learned. One of the episodes Jo remembers is doodling on paper while Miss Shepherd was speaking to the class. Miss Shepherd walked over to Jo's desk and told her that she was being rude for doodling while she was explaining a point. Jo objected, saying that she was still listening, but Miss Shepherd insisted that her behavior was rude. The amount of self-respect that Miss Shepherd showed was possible for a woman to have surprised Jo and is a memory that sticks with her to this day.

Miss Shepherd taught her students how good writing is structured and did not allow them to slacken off in that area. She had a level of integrity that brought out the best in her students, and it inspired Jo's respect, trust, and confidence. Even with this trust, however, Jo did not tell her favorite teacher about her hidden ambition to become a writer. Jo does treasure, however, a letter she received many years later from Lucy Shepherd, now retired from teaching and working in a bookstore in Bristol. The letter told Jo of how she had read *Harry Potter and the Philosopher's Stone*, and liked it. As Jo seems to hint at when she describes this letter, praise from an admired teacher can mean more than any medals or awards, even into adulthood.

Life outside of school during her teens was a challenge for Jo Rowling. Just like all the teens of the area, Jo suffered from the scarcity of recreational activities that were suitable for adolescents. Unlike London with its museums, concerts, clubs, and pulsing activity in general, Tutshill and Chepstow were pretty idle places for teens in their free time. There was not even a single-screen movie theater in town. Just like in any remote area anywhere, it was not unusual for teens to take up smoking cigarettes and loitering on street corners and other public places just for somewhere to be together and talk. Jo describes writing a lot in her room at Church Cottage, which was the furthest to the right on the second floor. At twelve, she wrote stories like "The Seven Cursed Diamonds," which readers now might notice has a similar image in the title to a philosopher's or a sorcerer's stone. Jo now claims the story contained no character or plot development. By the time she was a teenager daydreaming between stories, Jo admits to sitting on the windowsill of her room, smoking through the curtains, which her father would not have approved of, and dropping the cigarette butts out the window to the garden below. Perhaps as a teen she saw this act as mimicking the rebellion against her own father that Jessica Mitford showed when she ran away and charged a new camera to her father's account. Jo would often entertain her friends with stories that she made up when they sat together in the school cafeteria or wherever the kids could find to be together and talk.

Jo did participate in a student exchange trip with a school in France, near Lille, when she was 13, but even that proved to be uneventful. A friend of hers at the time described how they mocked the poor, run-down coal mining town where they had been sent as being one of the least exciting choices in France for young people to go. Another trip took Jo to see her first Shakespeare play, *King Lear*, at Stratford-on-Avon. Jo says the play fueled her enthusiasm for literature. During that same trip, her class also saw *The Winter's Tale*, in which Hermione is a famous character. In that play, Hermione, who has cleverly disguised herself as a statue for protection, comes back to "life" at the end. Only time will tell if any similarities to Shakespeare's Hermione will pop up for her namesake in the Harry Potter novels.

Sketching and music have been ongoing pleasures for Jo that continued during her years at Wyedean. As viewers of the BBC documentary "J. K. Rowling: Harry Potter and Me" can attest, Jo is a fairly good sketch artist. Her line drawings in pen and ink that she showed of Harry Potter, other characters, and scenes from the novels show an innate talent and not a little practice at the form. While the idea for Harry was still years away, sketching provided an early form of entertainment for the bored country girl living near the River Wye.

Musically, Jo learned to play guitar from her mother and could entertain herself plucking out a tune when she needed to relax. Years later she would describe the music she would most want to have with her on a deserted island. This included popular songs such as "Everybody Hurts" by REM; "Come Together" by The Beatles; "Big Mouth Strikes Again," by The Smiths (her favorite group reported in one interview); and Marianne Faithfull's "Guilt." As an adult, Jo would add classical music to her interests, teaching herself what she liked by listening to tapes. In the same interview about the deserted island music choices, Jo added Beethoven's *Appassionata* Piano Sonata; Tchaikovsky's Violin Concerto in D Major, and her favorite classical piece to date, Mozart's *Requiem Mass* in D Minor. It appears that Jo discovered the role classical music can play in aiding the imagination. When describing the *Appassionata* in the interview, she revealed that when hearing it she often imagined herself in a ball gown on a stage playing it for an intent and appreciative audience. Other classical pieces would bring memories back to her of the times when she encountered and savored them for the first time.

Among her peers at Wyedean Comprehensive in the 1970s, Jo found the popular American movie *Grease*, starring John Travolta and Olivia Newton-John, a fun diversion when it came out in 1978. Since Chepstow didn't have a theater, they had to go out of town to see it. Based loosely on the 1957 musical *West Side Story*, written by Arthur Laurents with music by Leonard Bernstein and lyrics by Stephen Sondheim, *Grease* was also set in the 1950s and involved two lovers from different gangs on opposite sides of the tracks. Both stories are modern adaptations of Shakespeare's *Romeo and Juliet*, another example of artistic borrowing of plots and characters. In *Grease*, just like in *West Side Story*, the audience is caught up in the story partly by the music and dancing and certainly by the age-old love story that highlights how opposites attract and love cuts through the toughest divisions, despite interference by peers and parents. John Travolta's greasy-haired Danny Zuko is the tough gang member with the black leather jacket, fast car, and loose character who also has a gentle side that longs for the sweet innocence of Olivia Newton-John's character, Sandy Ollson.

Characteristically, Jo apparently found an affinity with the female character Rizzo, played in the film by Stockard Channing and in a much later revival on Broadway by Rosie O'Donnell. Rizzo is the "bad girl," who has complex desires and defies society's "good girl" expectations, but is also attempting to hide a good deal of pain and low self-esteem through a tough exterior. Jo admits this was the mode she moved into herself at about this time, probably in an effort to defend herself against the pains that would come at home and the boredom outside in Chepstow. Rizzo, however, is also a more complicated character than the female romantic lead, Sandy, and probably attracted Jo because she was beginning to turn toward alternative tastes and away from naive sweetness, if she'd ever known much of that in the first place. Rizzo's famous song from the play and film is "Look at Me, I'm Sandra Dee," an indictment of "good girls" personified in 1950s popular culture by actresses such as blonde-haired Sandra Dee and Doris Day. Rizzo makes fun of these personalities who don't smoke, don't swear, and don't mix with people who are different from themselves. While seeming to admire the safe and protected place these girls live in with their pride intact, Rizzo not only lashes out at the way they look down their noses at a girl like her but also, and more important, criticizes society's double standard that expects more in terms of moral character and conviction of its women than it does of its men.

As an artist in the making, Jo knew the difference between accepting what is and questioning what could or should be, and this aspect of her adolescent personality led her to favor more alternative music, such as punk rock groups like The Clash. She even adopted the heavy black eye makeup that was popular with groups such as The Banshees, and this habit would stay with her well through college and into adulthood. Even her friends describe her during this period as Rizzo-like, smoking cigarettes, wearing heavy eye makeup and a trademark denim jacket, and exuding a tough exterior that masked a damaged self-esteem. Clearly, Jo was challenging the image expected of her as a studious member of the class of 1983.

Perhaps Rizzo's tough exterior and masked vulnerability also echoed an incident in Jo's experience at Wyedean when she had to stand up for herself against a bully. Bullies are a particular problem at school, where often academically gifted or serious students can be harassed by those who do not have the same ability or who do not care. Such was the case with Jo one day when she was attacked in the hall and thrown up against her locker by a girl in her class. Although she claims the lockers were the only thing holding her up, Jo fought back in self-defense. Though she saved herself and earned some level of peer respect for her efforts, she did not score any particular victories, and she still had to walk around school avoiding her attacker for some time afterwards.

Another experience of bullying that may have played into Jo's sensitivity to characters such as Draco Malfoy and his gang harassing the more gentle characters like Neville Longbottom was seeing a boy at Wyedean with very blonde, angel-like hair get picked on constantly because of his appearance. Still another involved an unnamed bully teacher that Jo says she had at one point and has described as the worst kind of teacher there is. There are certainly bully teachers at Hogwarts, as well as bully students. Clearly, school bullies are a vivid memory of school for Jo, and apparently their appearance in the Harry Potter novels has validated the very real and frightening experiences of many of her readers as well.

With disco all the rage in the 1970s, the adolescents struggling to find excitement at Wyedean did not even have a regular disco they could go to. Occasionally a disco was set up at the Drill Hall in Chepstow. Alternative rocker or not, Jo also enjoyed dancing and went to the disco at the Drill Hall for a few nights of fun that would spill over into similar nights out many years later in a more exotic location.

Also developing during her years at Wyedean was a mystery of a sort that would rock Jo's world at home. Pete had progressed well in his job at the Rolls-Royce factory in Bristol, and Anne continued to be well liked at Wyedean Comprehensive. When Jo was around twelve years old, about the same time she says she wrote "The Seven Cursed Diamonds," she remembers her mother having difficulty lifting a teapot, her first memory of what would become a serious illness that would affect every member of her family. The faculty in the Chemistry Department recognized something was wrong one day when Anne fell at school. The episodes continued and tests were run. Anne and Pete were told various things might be wrong and were sent home from doctors' offices time after time. It wasn't until Anne was thirty-four and Jo was fifteen that the diagnosis of multiple sclerosis, or MS, was finally delivered to them all. They were told that Anne had a particularly virulent strain.

The news came as a blow to all four members of the family. There is still no known cure for MS, and it can lead to death. It is a slow, debilitating disease that has its up and down days, until it takes a dive and allows its victim less normal movement than the day before. Watching an active woman in the prime of life lose control and eventually become unable to work, provide for the family she loves, or function normally brings a complicated array of emotions to her family, and Jo Rowling's was no exception. Jo has admitted that home became a hard place to stay because it was so difficult to watch her mother's physical condition deteriorate and be so helpless to fight against it. Pete nursed his wife faithfully and tended to her needs as she grew worse, but he could not replace her as the mother to the girls, who missed Anne's active sharing in their lives tremendously.

With home a place to try to get away from and the small village providing no place to go, Jo took up smoking and dove as deeply as she could into her alternative music, Gothic look, and her studies. It was a difficult time to be entering her last year of secondary school.

Jo points to the arrival in the school of a new student in Upper Sixth (or senior year in the United States) as coming to the rescue of her boredom and frustration. That student was Sean Harris, the son of an army man stationed at the base across the street from the school. Sean brought fresh ideas and new excitement to class. Like Jo, his accent was different from his classmates, and they both tended to feel a bit like outsiders. Jo found that they shared an interest in new wave music and humanitarian causes as well that made them fast friends. At 17, Jo was trying to achieve a dramatic, gritty attitude toward the realism of life, something, she says, she was influenced by Barry Hines's novel and film, *Kes*. Jo said in a television interview for the BBC and A&E's *Biography* that she also liked the way Sean turned a phrase when he talked, and she has admitted modeling much of Ron Weasley on him. She related that Sean was the first of her friends to pass his driving test, and what was even more important, Sean had a car, an old turquoise and white Ford Anglia. As any high school student from a small town knows, a working car with a licensed driver spells freedom and release from dull adolescent days. In a town surrounded by fields, Jo and Sean could drive off in the Anglia and feel they lived just a bit closer to the disaffected urban youth scene they so admired up north.

In the documentary on the BBC in late 2001, Jo introduces the audience to her "getaway driver and foul weather friend" to whom she dedicated the second Harry Potter novel, *The Chamber of Secrets*. In the interview, she and Sean stand beneath the Severn Bridge where they said they sat many a night sharing a cigarette and possibly a drink, commiserating about their lives, and dreaming of what they might do when they got out of Wyedean. Jo didn't drive and still has never learned, but Sean, with his cool looks and mannerisms, including a haircut in the style of the post-punk, New Romanticism band Spandau Ballet, would take her out of town frequently in the Anglia to clubs and discos in towns such as Bristol, Bath, or Cardiff. It was such a feeling of freedom to be able to leave the confines of their small town for a few hours. The blue Anglia came to symbolize rescue and escape for Jo, as she signals when she uses that color and model car as the flying car that rescues Harry from the Dursleys the summer before his second year at Hogwarts. When he and Ron miss the Hogwarts Express, the car takes them to Hogwarts in time for the start of school and lands in the Forbidden Forest. Sean Harris would be a friend through bad times more than once in Jo Rowling's life, as it turns out, but he would not need to rescue her again until some time later.

Perhaps with the security of a good friend helping her to stabilize her emotional life and cope with the problems at home and the boredom of living in a small town, Jo was voted head girl that year in school. This position at secondary school in England is held by one girl and one boy in their senior year. It is voted on by a combination of the faculty and the class, so it can be considered to be based on academic achievement and maturity, as well as popularity. It is more of an honorary and ceremonial position than a functional one. The head boy and girl usually host visiting guests at the school, and they may give a speech at an important event like graduation.

Two hardships in particular dimmed the brightness of what should have been a crowning senior year for Jo. One was that her mother was beginning to face the inevitable outcome of her disease. On April 23, 1983, at just thirty-eight years old and a few weeks before her first child's graduation, Anne made out her last will and testament. Working with her lawyer and friend, George Francis, she bequeathed all of her belongings to her husband, Pete. If he did not survive her, then half of her bequest would go to her sister Marian and brother-in-law Leslie and the other half to the Multiple Sclerosis Society. Later on, Jo Rowling would lend her influence to help raise money for the organization as well. One can only guess what kind of mood this put the family in as Jo neared graduation, a time that is usually marked by a sense of happiness and promise for the future.

The other disappointment for Jo was academic. Because she had done so well at Wyedean, the faculty recommended that she take the entrance exams required to apply at England's prestigious Oxford University. Oxford is comparable to an Ivy League school in the United States such as Harvard. It has a reputation for being attended—not exclusively, but often—by students from families of long-standing wealth, many of which have sent several generations to Oxford directly from expensive, private boarding schools. Admission standards are extremely high. For the faculty to recommend Jo try for Oxford was both a compliment to her intelligence and a challenge in every other way. Anne and Pete, who had not gone to college but who shared the hope that their girls would go, were delighted at the prospect.

Jo took the exams. They included her three languages of interest—English, French, and German. She scored an A in English and French and a B in German. She was denied admission to Oxford. Strangely, another girl who took the same tests at another school and scored only one A and two Bs in the same language tests was accepted. Rumors fly over seemingly unjust situations like this in the United States as well, but one of the perceptions at the time is certainly nothing new—charges of class bias over ability. The girl who got into Oxford took her exams at a private secondary school, whereas Jo took hers at state Wyedean. Though Jo has not spoken of this event in public, her disappointment and that of her parents and the staff at Wyedean must certainly have been great. It is difficult to imagine the lost opportunity not playing some role in influencing her attitude at Exeter that fall.

Not much has been written about Jo's graduation from Wyedean in 1983, but it is known that she has refused to come to class reunions ever since. Perhaps she links her years there with the sad days of her mother's illness. Perhaps that time draws a blank for her because of the long years of suffering boredom. She disliked the yellow and brown uniform of the school so intensely that she refuses to wear those colors again, even now as a mother approaching middle age. It should not be forgotten that these are the years that her characters are experiencing in the Harry Potter series. Harry, Ron, and Hermione are all going through these same difficult seven years of life, one year, one book at a time. Perhaps the reason Jo Rowling has not yet gone back is nothing more than that she needs to keep her own memories of those years from flooding back in new ways. A visit might trigger a memory that would upset the vision in her mind that she has set up for her ambitious project.

Jo's years at Wyedean represented some of her most successful and some of her most heartbreaking days. They also represented some of the most boring. While she graduated in the magical neighborhood of the Forest of Dean, with its owls and mushrooms and old tales of witches and spirits hovering over the leafy woods, changes were happening in the world as well.

In 1983, the year Jo Rowling graduated from high school, the first female astronaut, Sally Ride, rocketed into space. Alice Walker's *The Color Purple* won the Pulitzer Prize, and The Beatles, now long defunct and with John Lennon murdered two years earlier, released their *23 Number Ones* greatest hits album. Jan Mark, for *Handles,* won the Carnegie Medal that year in Britain, and in the United States, Cynthia Voigt's *Dicey's Song* won the Newbery Medal. The space shuttle *Challenger* made its maiden voyage that year, with no prediction in sight of its tragedy years later. In Beirut, a terrorist explosion killed 237 U.S. marines, and two days later Americans invaded Grenada. The films *The Big Chill* and *The Right Stuff* were hits at the box office. Beatles singer/songwriter John Lennon had already been gone for over two years, murdered in cold blood outside his New York City apartment building.

During the summer of 1983, a few short months after her mother had made out her last will and testament, eighteen-year-old Jo Rowling prepared to go to college. She chose Exeter, which was only a couple of hours away from home by car and even less by train. She packed books, sketch books, her guitar, long skirts, her favorite denim jacket, and lots of black eyeliner and mascara. She was ready to leave Wyedean and its rocky times behind, at least for a while. Years later, she would subject a cast of characters she had invented to their own travails at a secondary school of a very different kind that was anything but boring.

COLLEGE

Whether it was because she was away from home and the confines of her mother's illness and a small town, or whether it was because she was disappointed at going to her second-choice college, concentrating on a second-choice major, or some other reason or combination of these, Jo Rowling became a much different kind of student at Exeter. She often skipped classes, lost class handouts, and handed work in late, or not at all. Her active social life overtook academics as her first priority, and she made few strong impressions on her professors. Typical of her life's experience, many of her professors at Exeter do not remember her at all today.

Rather than major in English as her strong suit, Jo yielded to her parents' good intentions and took French, with the Classics, Greek and Roman studies. Practical Anne and Pete thought that their daughter might be able to find work as a bilingual secretary with a French degree, and that majoring in English would serve her in poorer stead.

Already Jo Rowling who had admired independent and politically active Jessica Mitford and liked to think of herself as idealistic and radical, couldn't have been more mistaken about finding that kind of thinking rampant in the hallways and greens at Exeter. Exeter was established in 1955, set on a hill overlooking the town of Devon. Typical of universities built in that time period in England and the United States, many of its buildings were nondescript in appearance, and the student body tended to be made up of young people from fairly conservative backgrounds, who tended to avoid challenging the status quo.

It took a while before Jo found fellow students who were willing to think deeply enough to challenge and experiment with some of the expectations the world seemed to have of them. Mostly, she found people who liked to frequent The Black Horse pub in town and the Devonshire House coffee bar on campus. They enjoyed her storytelling with them as the characters, just as her young friends on Nicholls Lane and those in the Wyedean cafeteria had before them. It's little wonder that Jo's storytelling skill has propelled her to unmatched popularity in the world as an author, when one considers the years of practice she had gaining friends through her stories.

In her tiny dorm room at Jessie Montgomery Hall or Lafrowda apartments, Jo would play her guitar, sketch, dream, and sometimes do a little French. At night she would go to The Black Horse pub with friends, see a movie (since there was a theater in town), or visit clubs. She admits that she did not apply herself to her studies, and Keith Cameron, one of her professors who would later become the head of the languages department, agrees that he saw her as an average student without a particular gift for languages evident in some of his other students. After she failed to register for a final exam, Jo was advised to drop Greek and Roman studies, which she had enjoyed especially for their mythological stories, for her last two years.

One break in the four-year routine of her less-than-inspiring college experience came when Jo spent her required third year in France. She taught English as a foreign language there for the year and thoroughly enjoyed her stay in Paris. It was her first experience with teaching as well. She was able to sample more cultures than just French because she shared an apartment with an Italian, a Russian, and a Spaniard. In Paris, she recalls reading Dickens's *A Tale of Two Cities* and crying at both the sadness and beauty of its closing line.

Back at Exeter, Jo continued working her way down her own self-selected reading list, running up an overdue fine at the campus library of $75 (£50). Though she says she initially read the series at age 14, J.R.R. Tolkien's *The Lord of the Rings* trilogy of fantasy novels—*The Fellowship of the Ring, The Two Towers*, and *The Return of the King*—apparently continued to influence her in college. Though written earlier, *The Hobbit*—an equally popular book thought to be the most accessible for children—is really the prequel to the series, and Jo has said she did not encounter it until she was in her twenties. Oddly enough, Jo would be linked with Tolkien thirty years later not only because of some of the similarities in their fantasy novel series, but also because the initial film releases of the first novels in their respective series debuted within days of one another in the fall of 2001.

In the late 1970s and early 1980s, fantasy games such as Dungeons and Dragons were quite popular pastimes with college students and young working professionals, who enjoyed intricate games, puzzles, whodunits, and fantasy and alternative worlds filled with adventure. *The Lord of the Rings* trilogy, originally published in 1954–1955, enjoyed a resurgence in popularity at the same time and often with these same people who enjoyed games. It is likely that Jo reread the novels during college and discussed them with her college classmates, and that these discussions may have stirred embers in her imagination.

John Ronald Reuel Tolkien (pronounced *tol-keen* with equal stress on both syllables) was born in 1892 and died in 1973. As often happens with literature, perhaps it was his death that precipitated the rebirth of interest in his novels on such a large scale. Others claim it was his strong advocacy for environmentalism, a movement that enjoyed a resurgence around the time of the oil embargo in the 1970s. Strangely, the hardback novels, which appeared in the 1950s were not printed again until 1965, the year J.K. Rowling was born, in pirated paperbacks. Their new accessibility and the resulting copyright dispute brought the attention of the American audience to these stories.

The novels' true devotees, however, hardly needed an event like Tolkien's death or renewed environmentalism to keep rereading and studying these vast, intricate novels. Many have been so deeply appreciative of and knowledgeable about the details of the various worlds, events, characters, and mythical creatures the books contain that they have developed an encyclopedic memory, drawn charts and graphs, and have enjoyed a lifelong hobby learning more about the associations and secrets in these fantastic worlds. Some readers adopted the fellowship mentality to such a degree that they faced being called cultist by those who did not appreciate their alternative lifestyles and interests.

Tolkien taught English literature and language at Oxford and was a linguist who invented more than a dozen completely new languages, some of which he used in his novels. At Oxford, he specialized in Old and Middle English, which can seem like different languages to contemporary readers unschooled in them. In his fiction, Tolkien created a world that existed in prehistoric times. He gave this world the Middle English name of Middle Earth. Tolkien worked out so many details of his imaginary world that readers who have come to love the novels feel an almost spiritual connection to Middle Earth, as though Tolkien told us all about a land that once actually existed and that we think we might remember in our collective consciousness if we only try hard enough.

One day while performing the less than stimulating task of grading papers, Tolkien, for reasons not even he understood, turned to a blank page in a student's examination booklet and wrote a short sentence that a hobbit lived in a hole. Since he had written stories, in addition to his scholarly work, Tolkien soon realized that he wanted to follow this hobbit down the hole, see why he lived there, and find out what a hobbit was in the first place. This curiosity to discover more about a character or vision is also evident in the works of Lewis Carroll and Jo Rowling, fueling their desire to write the stories to find out what would happen. Jo has described her following Harry in her imagination as akin to doing research rather than inventing. For his part, Tolkien finished his discovery or "research" by writing *The Hobbit*, which was published in 1937 as a story enjoyed by children then and today.

The Hobbit met with mixed reviews. Those who liked it very much included such powerhouses in the literary world as W.H. Auden and C.S. Lewis. Soon, Tolkien was urged to write a sequel. He had already started mapping out a sixteen-year history of Middle Earth, but it was evident before long that the story had matured, darkened, and deepened to a level that would take it beyond most children's comprehension and appreciation.

Grossly simplified, the stories are about the battle of good against evil, with the ring as a symbol of power that goes back and forth between the two forces. The fellowship is made up of Gandalf and his group of nine adventurous companions—including the main character, Frodo Baggins, a hobbit—who band together after a series of events in the first novel and set out to take the ring to the molten volcano of Mount Doom, where it will be destroyed. The novels contain elves, wizards, and other magical creatures, which don't always behave the way readers expect them to. These creatures have a solidity to their natures that makes them read absolutely true to themselves and the world Tolkien created for them.

Certainly the trilogy had its effect on the dreamy imagination of Jo Rowling, though only when the seventh and final Harry Potter novel is published can her series be compared with the Tolkien series to see where any similarities may lie. In his paid account of their time together, Jo's first husband claimed that she brought her own well-worn copy of *The Lord of the Rings* with her to Portugal.

So far, most readers call Harry Potter light by comparison to Tolkien's heavy, complicated themes and divined creations. Even Jo herself has said that she is not out to outdo Tolkien in any fashion and that his work involves completely new languages and mythologies that her magic world will not attempt to develop. Still, with the film of book two in the Tolkien series, *The Two Towers*, set to be released at the same time as book two in Rowling's series, *Harry Potter and the Chamber of Secrets*, the comparisons are likely to continue in people's minds for this reason if for no other.

During her last year at Exeter, Jo began a steady relationship with a fellow student that would linger on and off for years afterward. Her activities outside of class also included putting on the French play that last year, *The Agricultural Cosmonaut* by Obaldia. She worked on costumes, particularly for the character Clare, who was the cosmonaut. The advisor to the play remembers that Jo came to every rehearsal as one of the costume volunteers, but she was not one of those who performed on stage.

After completing her 3,000-word final essay in French and squeaking through final exams, Jo is reported to have graduated with a 2.2 out of a 4.0 grade point average in the spring of 1987. Even though she had not performed at her best, she had enjoyed herself, had a year's international experience, and had managed to finish college unscathed from her personal explorations.

Pete and Anne Rowling attended Jo's graduation, with Anne in a wheelchair. It was a proud moment for them to see their daughter accept her diploma from Chancellor Sir Rex Richards. That year, actress Glenda Jackson received an honorary doctorate degree, the same honor Jo would return to the college to receive over a decade later. Rowling would receive her first honorary doctorate degree in letters from Dartmouth College in the United States in 2000, but that future accomplishment, too, was not at all foreseeable on that spring day at Exeter in 1987. Pete and Anne Rowling had not had the opportunity to attend college themselves, and now their daughter was a college graduate. They probably knew her abilities and dreams lay in places yet unrecognized, but their chief concern was that Jo be able to find work and support herself on her own in the real world.

In the "real world" of 1987, Andy Warhol died and so did James Baldwin. Toni Morrison published *Beloved; Platoon* won the Oscar for Best Picture, and Prime Minister Margaret Thatcher won election for an unusual third term. Saddam Hussein apologized after an Iraqi missile landed on an American frigate, the *Stark,* in the Persian Gulf. The space shuttle program remained grounded after the *Challenger* disaster of just the year before. Susan Price won the Carnegie Medal for *The Ghost Drum,* and Sid Fleischman's *The Whipping Boy* won the Newbery Medal. The first four Beatles albums were released on compact discs.

This was the world in which college graduate Jo Rowling left Exeter to find a job that would support her secret desire of writing. As a newly educated young woman of the late twentieth century, she believed there was still a place for fantasy and a time for magic, and Jo set off, determined to find them.

Chapter 4

EARLY CAREER

Not only had education been important to Jo Rowling during her years growing up and becoming a young adult, but she would also eventually turn to education, where she had been so successful, in order to make a living. Just as actors do, writers often moonlight at various odd jobs until they break through with publication. Also, like acting, the writing profession rarely pays enough to cover all the bills, even when the writer is selling his/her work. However, Jo Rowling would soon leave her various odd jobs behind and join the fortunate few who are able to make a full-time living from creating their art. This would not happen, though, until she had lived through some uncertain and rocky times, and experienced tragic events that would shape her adulthood in a direction she probably never could have anticipated.

After graduating from Exeter in the spring of 1983, Jo moved to Clapham in southwest London and took a flat with some other women from college. At the urging of her parents, she enrolled in a bilingual secretarial course, utilizing her French and English. Her parents thought this would give her a practical skill that would put food on her table. One can only imagine what effect taking secretarial classes to prepare for a traditionally female, low-paying profession had on this young college graduate who admired rebels and activists like her hero, Jessica Mitford. However, Jo Rowling is not the first author to have paid her bills from doing secretarial work for others. At secretarial school, she learned to type at the speed of a professional. Jo admits this skill came in handy later when she typed her own manuscripts. Soon, she was "temping," filling in for full-time secretaries during their vacations, maternity leaves, extra workloads, etc. It is interesting that one of her temp jobs was with a publisher, where she was responsible for sending out rejection slips. Jo admits that she had neither the organizational talents nor an appreciation for secretarial work.

One job that provided some interest for her beyond securing a paycheck was with Amnesty International in London. Amnesty International is an international organization that advocates for human rights around the world. It was begun in 1961 by a British attorney, Peter Benenson, when he heard of two Portuguese students who were imprisoned for seven years for raising their glasses in a toast to freedom. In a tiny office in London and with a small group of volunteers, Benenson began writing letters and otherwise raising awareness about the plight of unfairly imprisoned people around the globe. Today, Amnesty International is the world's largest international human rights organization, with more than one million members and supporters in 144 countries and territories.

The United Kingdom branch of Amnesty International has its home offices in London, with branch offices in Edinburgh, Scotland, and Belfast, Northern Ireland. The offices in London are the research headquarters of the organization, where more than 300 staff members and 100 volunteers from 55 countries investigate cases that have been sought out by the organization or brought to its attention. The staff is made up of experts in law, medicine, the media, and technology. The specialists on the research staff are well regarded, and scholars, journalists, governments, and others frequently quote them when they come seeking information about human rights violations in various countries around the world.

Jo Rowling worked for the London research office, where she used her training in French and English to research human rights abuses in Francophone Africa. While the job fulfilled her desire for activism, soon the routine clerical nature of the day-to-day work discouraged her. Furthermore, she did not seem to fit in with the rest of the staff. Instead of going out to a pub for lunch with coworkers as was the custom in the office, Jo headed away from the group to cafes and other quiet places to work on one of two adult novels she was writing. Being the outsider did not go unnoticed. Never suspecting that Jo had ambitions beyond office work, her coworkers began teasing her that she must be having a lunchtime affair.

Besides stealing away at lunch hours to work on her writing, Jo found other ways to shield herself from the taxing world of office chatter and politics that can tear away at an artist's creativity. Often, she would type stories or other creative work instead of the material she was supposed to be typing. It probably amused her when her superiors and coworkers did not seem to notice the difference and she would get a few hours' worth of creative work done between her regular tasks. She used a similar technique when she worked as an audio secretary. This is a position where the secretary types what she hears dictated into headphones. Sometimes, instead of dictation, Jo substituted classical music and kept on typing her stories. Since her parents were not classical music buffs and she had had little exposure to it, Jo taught herself to enjoy classical music this way, trying different tapes until she found out what she liked. One of those she came to enjoy most was Beethoven's *Appassionata* piano sonata. When she didn't want to deal with idle and often petty office chatter, she'd throw on her headphones with Beethoven blasting in her ears and pretend she was very busy at her typewriter.

Sometimes the most creative ideas come when an artist is under pressure. Jo struggled with two novels for adults during the time she worked as a secretary, increasing her concentration, flexing her writing muscles, and devising a working method that would stand her in good stead later on.

While she worked at various office jobs in London, Jo's boyfriend from Exeter was living in Manchester, England, and encouraging her to move in with him there. Jo had been taking the monotonous, 250-kilometer (150-mile) train ride back and forth from London to Manchester to visit him on weekends. One of these boring train rides back to London in June 1990 would prove to be one of the most inspirational and productive few moments of her creative life. On this ride, the character of Harry Potter stepped aboard the train with her and settled into her imagination. While the joy of meeting Harry Potter changed her creative life forever, things still progressed awkwardly in her personal and professional life for quite some time, and just six months later tragedy would dim the light of discovering Harry.

Jo finally acquiesced to her boyfriend and moved to Manchester in 1990. She got a secretarial job at the Manchester Chamber of Commerce but was soon laid off. She also worked at Manchester University, but she says she was not happy in that job either. It is indicative of Jo's self-alienation from the working world on which she depended for a living at this time that the Manchester Chamber of Commerce can show no record of her having worked there. Employees with more than twenty years of service at the Chamber do not remember her, even after her Harry Potter fame brought people in asking if the workers there knew her when she had begun putting notes of the early stages of Harry Potter into a shoebox. Interestingly, this lack of making a lasting impression marks much of her school years as well, a time in training, perhaps, for the fight for privacy that would plague her many years later when Harry Pottermania drove her to protect her private life and writing time from the demands of a curious world.

While Jo was seemingly tossing about from job to job and place to place, her mother's health was deteriorating rapidly. Jo went home to Church Cottage in Tutshill just before Christmas 1990 and remembers her mother looking tired and thin when she saw her. Anne's illness had been taking its toll for so long, however, that Jo did not realize that her condition had made a marked shift. Jo said goodbye to her mother on Christmas Eve and, as many independent adults in their mid-twenties do, left to spend the rest of the holiday with her boyfriend and his relatives.

On New Year's Eve at 7:30 in the morning, Jo was awakened and told that her father was on the phone. This was not something Pete would normally do, so she immediately thought of her mother and the definite possibility that the news they had all been fearing for ten years had come. Anne Rowling had the dignity of dying peacefully at home just a few days after Jo last saw her.

Although Church Cottage sat next to a cemetery, Anne Rowling preferred to be cremated, and her service was held at a crematory in Gloucester, some thirty miles away from Tutshill. The service was intimate, with only a few family members and friends present. Anne's sister, Marian, and her brother-in-law, Leslie, were held up in traffic and arrived too late for the ceremony. Grieving the loss of their beloved Anne, these lost opportunities to say goodbye only magnified the sadness of all concerned.

Losing one's mother is a traumatic and cutting blow no matter when it happens. The feeling of being orphaned is not blunted even when the surviving offspring is no longer a child. As the person who first introduced her to the wonder of books through her own love of reading, Jo's mother has an intimate connection to Jo's creative work that goes beyond the normally close and complex personal ties of most mother and daughter relationships. Anne's long illness also played a factor in spurring Jo to write, since one can easily envision Jo turning even deeper toward books and writing as an escape and an outlet from the emotions she must have experienced as a result of the difficulties of her mother's debilitating disease. A creative response on the part of a daughter is not unusual to a mother's untimely death. Other popular culture, contemporary artists, for example, such as singer/songwriter Madonna and comedian Rosie O'Donnell, have spoken out about the influence of their mothers' early deaths on their lives, their chosen methods of creative expression, and the way they have handled their success.

One of the interesting effects of Anne's early death on Jo might be observed from the central act of love in *Harry Potter and the Sorcerer's Stone*. The villain, Voldemort, killed Harry's parents when he was an infant. As the story is told in the first novel, Voldemort first killed Harry's father then went after Harry. Harry's mother died trying to save her child. Voldemort's powers and physical form were diminished when his efforts to kill Harry failed. Harry was the child that lived, and his story became legend, making him famous in the world of wizards and witches. When Harry learns all this much later at Hogwarts School of Witchcraft and Wizardry, he is told that he gained his power from his mother's sacrifice. He was able to defy Voldemort because his mother loved him enough to die saving him. So far in the novels, this degree of love seems to overpower any of the evil that has yet arisen. That makes the love of a mother quite important, and the love of a martyred mother, one who went too soon, even stronger.

In *Harry Potter and the Sorcerer's Stone*, Harry sees his mother, whom he does not remember because she died so soon after he was born, in the Mirror of Erised—desire, spelled backwards. The Mirror of Erised shows those who look in it not a picture of the future as readers might first expect, but instead it shows them what they most want to see. Most readers, and Jo Rowling herself, acknowledge that the loss of Harry's parents and his relationship to them constitute the emotional center of the novels. Jo has admitted that the mirror scene in book one of the series is her favorite and was inspired by the loss of her own mother. Possibly the further wound caused by lost chances to say goodbye fuels this scene where Harry has the opportunity to see and speak to his parents, who can see but not speak to him.

When asked what she would say to her mother if she could speak to her in a Mirror of Erised for a few short minutes like Harry does, Jo Rowling says that she would tell her about the daughter she had three years later, about her books, and about so many other things that happened to her after her mother died. Like a typical child, she notes, she would use up their time sharing all of her news and updating her mother on her stories, and not think to ask her mother until it was too late the universal question that she should have asked had she been thinking properly—the question of what it is really like to be dead.

In the film version of *Harry Potter and the Philosopher's/Sorcerer's Stone*, only one scene was added that does not appear in the book, and that was the scene depicting Voldemort killing Harry's mother with Harry in her arms. Voldemort is a shadowy figure that the camera captures from behind, and the scene is shot from below and outside a muggle house window. The audience sees Harry's mother, with long red hair, the same woman from the Mirror of Erised, holding a baby wrapped in a blanket, being attacked by some force from Voldemort, and falling. Some observers who look for clues for the advancement of the plot have pointed out that

Harry's parents were living in muggle housing, or at least housing that was very muggle-like, rather than wizard-like, in appearance in the film. It is known that Chris Columbus and some of the actors and others were told a few of the future plot details by Jo. Only novels five to seven will reveal the importance, if any, of the setting of Lily Potter's death.

Losing her mother shook Jo Rowling's already rocky world. Among other things, her sagging relationship with her boyfriend in Manchester suffered even more. One night she left after an argument and checked into a hotel in Didsbury, a Manchester suburb. Again, pressures from the outside world activated her imagination, and Jo spent much of that night trying to think of something else. That something else was the game of Quidditch, which she spent most of the night inventing and which would go on to be so popular with both wizards and readers of the Harry Potter series. When she was deciding what name to give Harry's muggle aunt and uncle, she once thought about using Didsbury, but then she liked Quidditch too much to name the Dursleys after the town where she had invented it.

Another difficulty that arose shortly after her mother's death was that her flat in Manchester was robbed. Among the things stolen were all of the sentimental objects that Anne had left to Jo. Losing her mother and these few meaningful gifts to remember her by nearly in a single stroke was too much for the young writer. Her relationship with her college sweetheart was over as well. It seemed like the best thing to do was to leave Manchester, and England—much as her hero, Jessica Mitford, had done many years before.

Steve Cassidy, principal of the Encounter English Schools in Oporto, Portugal, had placed an ad for English teachers in the *Guardian* newspaper. Jo answered the ad, sending in her resume and contact information, and Cassidy interviewed her at a hotel near the Leeds railway station. According to Cassidy, Jo had a rather gothic appearance when he met her that did not make her a prime candidate for a teacher at his school. She still wore the heavy black eye makeup, now accompanied by an even more mournful look.

Oporto is the second largest city in Portugal, and it is best known for its tourist industry, revolving around its famous port wines. Tourists come to Oporto to sample port at the wineries of companies such as Taylor's and Graham's. Henry the Navigator came from Oporto, and it is possible, though not yet definitively verified by historians, that Ferdinand Magellan, the famous explorer who made the first voyage around the world, may have been born in Oporto as well.

When Jo got the job and headed off for Portugal with few possessions in tow except her notes for the beginnings of *Harry Potter*, her father and sister Di were also in different locations. Pete Rowling had left Church Cottage with its intimate memories of his years of struggle in caring for his ill wife and moved to a new house in Chepstow. Di lived in Edinburgh, Scotland, working as a nurse. Jo welcomed the fresh start that the move to Portugal signaled, and she settled into the accommodations provided by the school, a four-bedroom apartment that she would share with fellow teachers. The apartment was above a drugstore, the Farmacia da Prelada, on the rua Central de Francos.

Jo shared the apartment with Aine Kiely and Jill Prewett, both in their mid-twenties. Luckily for Jo, she got along well with her two flatmates right away. Aine Kiely was an Irish woman from Cork with a fun-loving personality. Jill Prewett was English with a strong sense of individuality. While these two women were good friends of Jo's in Oporto, they would become even better friends when Jo found she could rely on them later when things went bad for her. She dedicated *Harry Potter and the Prisoner of Azkaban,* book three in the series, to these two women, whom she referred to in the dedication as the godmothers of Swing. Swing is the name of a disco that the three frequented in Oporto, looking for fun and male companionship after their classes ended for the night.

Jo taught English in night school, from approximately 5:00 P.M. to 10:00 P.M. weeknights, and then again on Saturday mornings. Her students were predominantly teenagers, ages fourteen to eighteen, who came in for help in studying for exams. Jo says these were her favorite students because they were not afraid to voice their opinions and were excited about the future, which they approached with many new ideas. Although Jo says she also taught students as young as eight and as old as sixty-two at the school, including businesspeople and homemakers, she became head of the department in charge of teaching the teens.

Teaching night school left most days free for her writing, and, since she did not have an early morning class, her nights could go quite late with socializing and drowning the sorrows of her recent losses. The hours suited her, and she quickly resumed her habit of writing in cafes during the day. The Cafe Majestic was one of her known favorites. It was her practice to write in longhand during the day in a cafe and then get to the Encounter School early before class to type up the notes she had made that day. While Oporto is not famous for its exotic flair, its difference from Tutshill, Exeter, London, and Manchester had its effect on Jo. She seemed to relax and enjoy the warm climate, green parks, and the Ribeiro, the Riverside.

One night as the trio of friends haunted local nightclubs, they happened to go into the Meia Cava. There were two floors to the bar, with disco playing upstairs and jazz downstairs. When the three women walked into the downstairs area, a journalism student by the name of Jorge Arantes spotted Jo and liked her immediately. Her red hair and blue eyes, so different from most native Portuguese women, stood out. They began talking in English and soon realized that their mutual love of books attracted them to one another beyond mere physical appearance. According to Arantes, who sold his version of their story once Jo became well known, they talked for at least two hours that first night and gave each other their telephone numbers.

Jorge called Jo two days later, again according to his account. They agreed to go out together, and soon afterwards their relationship became exclusive. Unfortunately, according to friends and family, the relationship suffered from jealousy almost from the start on one side or the other, so that dramatic arguments and romantic make-ups became a frequent and unhealthy cycle in Jo and Jorge's relationship.

The couple moved in together, along with Jorge's aging mother, Marilia Rodrigues, in a small two-bedroom house. Moving in with one parent for a while is common in Portugal, and though Jorge's mother had very little in common with Jo, she claims that she welcomed Jo into her home.

Jorge has told in his paid story that Jo was reading Jane Austen and a worn copy of Tolkien's *The Lord of the Rings* that she'd brought with her from England and continued to work on her Harry Potter series throughout their relationship. He claims that she had plotted out all seven Harry Potter books by then and was working hard with his encouragement. Other claims by Arantes, such as the degree of his influence on the writing, have been vehemently denied by Jo.

Jorge claims he proposed to Jo on August 28, 1992, and they were married on October 16, 1992. Interestingly, and perhaps foreshadowing the trouble that lay ahead, Jo wore black on her wedding day. She is not smiling in her wedding photograph, in which she stands with Jorge amid his family. In *Harry Potter and the Prisoner of Azkaban*, Professor Trelawney, who teaches Divination class, warns one of Harry Potter's classmates, Lavender Brown, that the event she has been dreading will take place on Friday, October 16. Given the way her marriage would eventually turn out, it is unlikely to be a coincidence that Jo gives the exact date and day of her first wedding for the event Lavender has been dreading.

Soon after the wedding, Jo became pregnant. She remained teaching at the Encounter English School and still occasionally went out evenings with Aine and Jill to share the day-to-day details of her pregnancy, as well as matters they had in common from the classes they were teaching. Jo's relationship with Jorge remained strained and tumultuous, particularly when he would go out with his friends and she would go out with hers.

One feature of the pregnancy that Jo remembers well is that she listened to Tchaikovsky's violin concerto almost every day. She had given it to Jorge for his birthday but somehow adopted it as a score to the days and months she spent teaching, writing, and dealing with her complicated role as wife, writer, teacher, and expectant mother. When women are glad to be pregnant, the time they carry their babies can be very special, intimate, and memorable to them. They know that they will never be quite as close to their children again as they are when they share all the same experiences in such an intimate space. Jo says that to this day when she hears Tchaikovsky's concerto it always reminds her of her daughter.

Jo admits that the best thing to happen to her during her marriage to Jorge, and indeed the best moment of her life—including the publication of her world-famous books—was the birth of her daughter, Jessica, on July 27, 1993, four days before Jo's twenty-eighth birthday. Jo delivered Jessica in the Maternidade Julio Dinis nursing home after seven hours of labor. Interestingly, if Jessica had been a boy, she would have been named Harry. Instead, Jo says she named her after her hero, Jessica Mitford.

Unfortunately, a newborn baby usually adds strain to an already weak relationship, and that was exactly what happened when Jo brought Jessica home to live with Jorge. The couple had depended more on Jo's income than on Jorge's job in the National Service, so money was tight. Arguments raged, and tempers flared. Further complicating the couple's relationship, a bizarre accident necessitating an almost one-month stay in Hospital de Sao Joao left little Jessica with circulation trouble in a toe that nearly required amputation. Soon, by many eyewitness accounts and even some versions of Jorge's own story, domestic violence became a painful reality in Jo's life. On November 17, 1993, in a row that was witnessed even by their neighbors, Jorge threw Jo out of the house, keeping baby Jessica inside with him.

If an intelligent young woman can imagine a worse scenario than being thrown out on the street in a foreign country without her child and with no belongings except the clothes on her back, that scenario still would be hard put to rival Jo Rowling's reality in late 1993. She knew the marriage was over, but she also knew that she had to get Jessica.

She turned to her friends Aine and Jill for help, and they called other friends, who offered her police assistance and a safe place to stay. The next day, Jo went back to the flat with the police and asked Jorge to give her the baby. The police officer could not legally make him hand Jessica over. Whether Jorge knew that at the time or not, the scene he and Jo created on the street in front of the neighbors, with the police there and the baby crying, eventually resulted in his giving the baby over to her. Two weeks later, Jo and Jessica left Oporto, never to return.

Unfortunately, leaving Portugal did not end the problems Jo experienced in the years before Harry Potter became known to the world. However, Harry Potter was with her in the notes and pages she carried with her from England to Portugal and back, sustaining her creative life and spirits all through this time. She continued to be dedicated to the story of this lonely boy who did not know he had a great history and magical powers beyond his imagination. Perhaps these years were her Dursley years with Harry, when it didn't seem like life offered much hope or kindness or any sign of a future.

With Anne gone, Jo in Portugal, and Di in Scotland, Pete Rowling remarried on April 2, 1993. He was 48 and married his former secretary, a woman eight years younger than he, named Janet Gallivan. The small ceremony occurred less than two years after Anne's death. They settled in Pete's new house in Chepstow, just about two miles from Church Cottage. Rumors lingered about Pete and Janet's relationship in the months that followed Anne's death. For his part, Pete had nursed his ill wife faithfully, according to all concerned. Janet, it has been said, left a husband and two sons in Bristol to be with him.

There is also speculation about whether or not Jo and Di harbored or continue to harbor any resentment toward their father for his remarriage. Much is made of Jo's dedicating the first Harry Potter book to her mother, sister, and daughter but not mentioning her father. There is at least one Peter in the novels who is a villain. If there were tough times in Jo's relationship with her family, it seems that they have been smoothed over more recently. Both Pete and Janet attended the July 2000 ceremony when Jo received an honorary doctorate at her alma mater, Exeter. There is at least one photo of her with her characteristic grin, embracing both of them. They were also, it is reported, in attendance at her second wedding in December 2001. For whatever reason, best known by the family themselves, Jo did not appear to seek out her father in her time of need in terms of finding a place to stay. Perhaps it was pride; perhaps it was discomfort with his new relationship. Jo has never spoken of a rift, and when questioned about it, she dismisses the notion, implying it is either none of people's business, which it isn't, or that her family, like most others, went through a temporary edginess in their relationship following the death of a loved one, and it should not be taken as anything more than that.

Back in December 1993, however, Jo Rowling was still a long way off from honorary degrees and happy second marriages. She took Jessica to Scotland and spent the holidays with her sister Di and Di's new husband in Edinburgh, trying to figure out the rest of her life. Jo's sister Di had married Roger Moore on September 3, 1993, at the St. Andrew Registration Office, India Buildings, in Edinburgh. Jo's predicament was the second time in three years that tragedy had struck Jo during the holidays. She had no job; she had a six-month old baby, and the political and social climate in the United Kingdom had turned ungenerous and unforgiving of single parents in trouble.

British Prime Minister John Major had addressed the Conservative Party Conference at Blackpool in October that same year. In his speech, he argued that single mothers were to blame for the problems of young people in England. The speech still resonated two months later when Jo arrived at her sister's small flat at 140 Marchmont Road in Edinburgh, and Jo speaks of it often now when she talks about the cause of supporting single mothers in need. She says that she already felt terrible about her situation and didn't need the government making her feel like a second-class citizen for making mistakes in her life when she wanted desperately to do better and set things right for herself and her daughter.

When Jo and her baby arrived in crisis, Di and her husband, Roger, took them in, but everyone concerned knew that it was not a good idea for a newly separated mother and her infant to live in a confined space with a newlywed couple. In the warmth of her sister's and her daughter's close affections, however, Jo thought out a plan to pull herself back together. She would find a place to live in Edinburgh, since she liked the city very much, and she would find a job teaching. If she had to go on public assistance temporarily while all of this got worked out, she would rather do that than burden her sister and her brother-in-law any further in their fresh new lives together.

The process of getting government aid was humiliating for Jo, who was, after all, a proud woman of 28 with a college degree and work experience. She did accept a loan from her close friend from Tutshill, Sean Harris, but this was only a drop in the very deep bucket needed to support her and her daughter. A meager subsistence was finally approved by the government, and Jo was awarded approximately $103.50 (or £69) per week to live on. This didn't buy much, but by luck and will, she was able to rent an unfurnished, one-bedroom flat in Gardens Crescent in Leith, which is in the old, but not worst, area of Edinburgh. This address would become famous a few years later as the place where she lived on welfare at least part of the time while raising her daughter and, finally if not quite remarkably, the place where she was living when she finished her manuscript for *Harry Potter and the Philosopher's Stone*. Jo and Jessica lived in the tiny apartment for about six months.

Through the early months of 1994, Jo found herself in the depths of depression and sought counseling. Readers of *Harry Potter and the Prisoner of Azkaban*, book three in the series, remember the Dementors as frightening creatures that can suck out all joy and memories of any good thing and leave their victims empty with despair. This is territory that Jo can write about with personal knowledge, since this is the state of mind in which she spent much of her time during those few months. It is interesting to read book three with the idea of depression and counseling in mind. One can easily see how the treatments supplied to Harry by his various wizard professors mimic therapy methods to varying degrees.

By the summer of 1994, Jo's vision of her future was beginning to clear. She filed for a divorce from Jorge on August 10. Di's husband, Roger, had formed a business partnership in town called The Sint Partnership, and they had purchased a cafe, called Nicolson's, which was near the corner of South Bridge and Royal Mile, not too far from Jo's apartment. Jo resumed her habit of writing in cafes, this time with her baby daughter in tow. She'd take Jessica out for a walk in her stroller, then push the stroller into the cafe when Jessica fell asleep and work quietly at a corner table, nursing a cup of coffee. Since her brother-in-law owned the business, the staff didn't bother her for staying in the cafe for long periods, buying little food or drink. They basically left her alone.

Jo's usual table was a window seat, where she could muse and look down on the street below. Perhaps a sign of encouragement to her as she worked there was the name of a street near Nicolson's, Potterrow. She wrote her manuscript in longhand, mostly in notebooks, and sometimes brought a book to read if she were stuck for a moment and needed to think out Harry's next move.

When she wasn't writing, she was either taking classes, student teaching to gain her teaching certificate in Scotland, tending to Jessica, or looking for work or child care so that she could get a job. She has said in interviews that the one thing she let go during these times was the cleanliness of her apartment. She admits to not being a good housekeeper. Her sister and friends had lent her scraps of furniture and a few necessities, and the apartment was dreary enough before that. Particularly painful, says Jo, was seeing how many toys her friends' children had and having to give her daughter used toys that were often not in good condition. She kept herself and her daughter warm and fed, but toys were a luxury she simply could not afford. At one time, the number of toys Jessica owned could fit into a shoebox. Jo says that she would sometimes pick up very part-time secretarial work to supplement her benefits. She found herself, however, in a difficult situation when it came to child care. She couldn't afford to go off benefits completely because she couldn't earn enough money to live on and pay for child care at the same time. When she applied for help with Jessica, she was told that Jessica was too well cared for, that the money available had to go to children with even greater need. While today Jo says she understands this problem, she also points out there is a crack in the system that does not allow single mothers with children to move up incrementally in a way that could bring them out of dire financial circumstances.

By the summer of 1995, Jo received a helping hand from a couple of places that brought her up over the edge and out of the black hole of poverty. One was a monetary gift from a person who remains anonymous that paid for child care for Jessica so that Jo could return to school full time and gain her teaching certificate. The other was a grant from the Scottish Office of Education and Industry. Jo's divorce from Jorge was finalized on June 26, 1995, and she obtained permanent custody of Jessica without Jorge's interference. All of these factors together began to build momentum for Jo's future.

Her future, as she saw it then, was to gain her certificate and return to teaching full time. Finishing her manuscript and having it accepted by the Christopher Little Literary Agency and then by Bloomsbury, a British publisher, against incredible odds, coincided with her student teaching in Edinburgh. Having lived through the hard realities of life, Jo Rowling had no illusions about fame and fortune in terms of her book. She would be happy to see it in print, but she knew not to count on that to secure the future of herself and her daughter.

By July 1996, Jo had attained her first goal, graduating as a teacher. She had moved herself from a 2.2 grade point average in French at Exeter to a D-, then a B, from tutor Michael Lynch in her first student teaching experience at St. David's Roman Catholic High School in Dalkeith, to all A's from her tutor, Eilane Whitelaw, at her next position at Leith Academy. After obtaining her teaching certification, Jo registered her name with the General Teaching Council and was offered a teaching assignment at Leith Academy, just a few yards from where she lived. The situation at Leith, one of Scotland's oldest schools, was particularly beneficial for her not only in terms of its location, since Jo didn't drive, but also since Leith offered on-site daycare, where she could place Jessica during the day.

In addition to the on-the-job training methods she used with her Portuguese students in Oporto, Jo had learned in Edinburgh to be a teacher who used her imagination in her classroom to make lessons more interesting for herself and her students. After her lackluster first performance at student teaching, Jo turned herself around, realizing that she had to pass the course to provide a new life for herself and her daughter in Edinburgh. Rather than teach strictly from the textbook with monotonous lesson plans, she often made up games and other creative activities for the students to help them with their French. One such game involved cards with pictures that she drew herself. On one side would be the sketch she drew and on the other the words for that picture in French. Students would be asked to make sentences using two of the cards, and keeping cards became a reward system in the game for constructing the sentence correctly.

One incident that Jo has described shows how her dual lives of writer and teacher continued to fuse and separate during her teaching days. As most teachers have encountered on many more occasions than they care to count, one day a student arrived in class with no paper and no pen or pencil to do the work at hand. Jo scolded her for being unprepared and told her to go up to her desk and get some paper. While Jo walked around the room checking other students' work, she didn't notice at first that the student lingered at Jo's desk a while longer than she should have. Finally, when Jo asked her to sit down, the student, who was named Maggie, asked Jo if she was a writer. Embarrassed that her student had obviously seen the scribblings on her desk, Jo remembers muttering something about it being just a hobby.

Guilt over writing instead of doing any other practical money-making job while teaching hung over Jo's days even then. On the one hand, she knew that she should be giving full effort to teaching to ensure the financial stability of herself and her daughter, but she could never seem to give herself over completely to anything but writing. Her stories drove her, it is clear, and everything else paled in comparison.

While she was still searching for a permanent teaching position after graduation—after the manuscript for *Harry Potter and the Philosopher's Stone* had been accepted by Bloomsbury but had not yet gone to print—Jo received a writer's grant of $12,000 (£8,000) in the form of the Scottish Arts Council Book Award. This was enough to live on while working on the other books and seeing book one into publication. It is small wonder that Jo Rowling has such a devotion to Scotland even to this day. She has the satisfaction of having earned her way to a teaching career there that enabled her to house, clothe, and feed herself and her daughter, while at the same time, Scotland's generosity in the arts freed her from having to dream up exciting lesson plans ever again (except by the professors of Hogwarts!).

On June 26, 1997, *Harry Potter and the Philosopher's Stone*, the British title of book one, was published in hardcover by Bloomsbury. They printed only 500 copies of the book. Jo's joy at seeing the book in print was rivaled only by the birth of her daughter. Within three days, Jo received a phone call from her agent telling her that the American rights to the book were being auctioned off. Arthur Levine of Scholastic Books was very interested. Her agent would keep in touch.

The next phone call Jo Rowling received would change her financial status forever. It appeared that she would never have to worry about getting another job or having enough money again. The long years of struggle in her personal and professional lives were about to be rewarded by the little boy who walked into her imagination on that boring train ride from Manchester to London in 1990. That little orphan boy with the scar on his forehead was about to work more magic in the world than anyone, perhaps even Jo Rowling herself, had thought possible.

Author Joanne Rowling poses in a New York bookstore, Oct. 17, 1998. Rowling, the author of Harry Potter and the Sorcerer's Stone, *has ridden to the top of bestseller lists in Britain and the United States with her engaging children's book about Potter, a bespectacled 11-year-old prodigy. (AP Photo/Suzanne Mapes)*

Author J.K. Rowling, right, and partner Neil Murray, left, arrive at the world film premiere of Harry Potter and the Philosopher's Stone *screened at the Odeon Cinema in London's Leicester Square, Nov. 4, 2001. (AP Photo/Richard Lewis)*

J.K. Rowling, author of a fourth Harry Potter novel, signs a copy for Nick Drews, 10, at a children's breakfast in New York, Oct. 20, 2000. Drews is one of 10 winners who submitted an essay entitled "How the Harry Potter Books Changed My Life," to a contest sponsored by the publisher. Rowling announced that her fifth novel in the series, Harry Potter and the Order of the Phoenix, *would probably not be ready by July 2001. (AP Photo/Louis Lanzano)*

Britain's Queen Elizabeth II meets Harry Potter creator J.K. Rowling, center, and Senior Commissioning Editor Emma Matthewson, right, looking at a Harry Potter manuscript at Bloomsbury Publishing in London, March 22, 2001. During the so-called royal "theme day," the Queen is due to see various aspects of the book industry. (AP Photo/PA/Stefan Rousseau, Pool)

Chapter 5

THE LIFE OF HARRY POTTER

If, a few years ago, someone had predicted that a brand new series of books would sell more than 150 million copies in 50 languages over five years at the turn of the millennium, the subject of those books would have been of great curiosity, debate, and speculation. Perhaps it might be science fiction, dealing with life on Mars. Perhaps a self-help book about how to live well into one's 100s. Maybe a great popular philosopher would arise with good advice about finding happiness. It seems quite likely, even probable, that no one, even J.K. Rowling herself, could have predicted that it would be the story of an eleven-year-old orphan boy who didn't know he was a wizard. What is it about the Harry Potter novels that has struck such a chord with children and adults alike? What is it about his story that entices readers to want to know what will happen next and stand in line for the first copies of each new installment? There is something about this character and his cohorts, their setting at school, and the fast-moving plot that captures the interest of people in these times like at no other time before. Sociologists, psychologists, and other specialists try to understand what has come to be called the "Harry Potter Phenomenon," even as it continues to unfold. It will take many years after the seventh and final book in the series is released before sound analyses can begin. In the meantime, Harry Potter's life, just like the life of his creator, is running full steam ahead.

BEGINNINGS

The year 1990 marked the arrival of the last decade of the millennium. In the world, it was the year Iraq invaded Kuwait and the year former USSR head Mikhail Gorbachev won the Nobel Peace Prize. Nelson Mandela was freed from his prison cell in South Africa. A Van Gogh painting brought a record $82.5 million at auction. *Dances with Wolves*, starring Kevin Costner, won the Academy Award for Best Picture that year; *Wolf* by Gillian Cross won the Carnegie Medal, and Lois Lowry's *Number the Stars* won the Newbery. Paul McCartney released *Tripping the Live Fantastic*, which contains nostalgic covers of many Beatles songs played live during his *Flowers in the Dirt* tour in 1989. NASA launched its famous Hubble Telescope that would allow astronomers to peer deeper into space than ever before.

Maybe it's helpful to think of how Harry Potter first arrived in the imagination of Jo Rowling that summer day in 1990. She was sitting on a train, taking a familiar ride back to London after visiting her boyfriend in Manchester. They had spent the weekend looking for an apartment. Her boyfriend had been asking her to move to Manchester so that they could be closer, but at that time Jo still had to get back to London to start a new week at work.

She had taken the same 40-minute, 150-mile train ride many times before and had no particular reason to be excited or full of creative energy or mental stimulation that day. In fact, she was a bit bored. The train was delayed and had not been moving for a while. In all, the delay would cause the 40-minute ride to take four hours. Jo Rowling sat looking out the window at some cows, when Harry Potter, in the form of an eleven-year-old boy with disheveled black hair, green eyes, and broken round glasses, walked into her imagination. She knew he was a boy who thought himself to be normal, but he was on a train to go to a boarding school for wizards. As soon as she saw him, she knew he was a wizard but that he didn't know his own true identity or that he was very powerful. She knew he was an orphan, too, but she didn't know why or how. She sat looking at him in her mind's eye, and ideas began to pour in almost faster than she could sort them. It was as though she had been put under a magical spell, or like the mail call at Hogwarts when hundreds of owls come rushing in, or the beginning of *Harry Potter and the Philosopher's/Sorcerer's Stone* when the letters inviting Harry to Hogwarts flood in by the hundreds through every possible opening in the Dursley house. Jo says that she had never felt that level of excitement over the arrival of a creative idea before. The encounter was like meeting a new person and hitting it off right away; you knew you were going to like this person and wanted to know more about him. She says the excitement of meeting Harry for the first time was a physical rush, a feeling that left her light-headed and full of anticipation for exploring their new relationship; she has said it felt quite a bit like falling in love.

Like most writers, published or not, Jo Rowling normally carries pen and paper with her to jot down ideas. Strangely, rummaging through her bag, she could only find a pen that didn't work. She didn't have a pencil either, or even, she has said, an eyeliner, or anything she may have used in a pinch to write with, so she ended up watching and thinking about all of the details that were entering her mind instead of immediately trying to catch them and write them down. She says now that the fact that she sat back in her seat and let herself dream and remain open to Harry's world might be why so many ideas found their way to light so quickly. She relaxed and let herself believe that if she didn't remember a stray detail here or there, it probably wasn't worth remembering anyway.

As the train lurched forward and chugged along, the summer countryside between Manchester and London moving past, she found herself meeting not only Harry but also Ron Weasley, Hagrid, Nearly Headless Nick, and Peeves in the world of her imagination. A building also came into view in her mind, a castle the likes of which she had never seen before—Hogwarts School of Witchcraft and Wizardry. She knew that it stood in a remote place away from the city, and she decided that it must be located in Scotland. There was something about her parents meeting and falling in love on a train going to Scotland that echoed this whole experience for her, though that probably didn't occur to her then. During that train journey, Jo Rowling discovered that the story she was envisioning would take seven books to tell. She kept dreaming and seeing and thinking all the way back to London, but she didn't write down anything until she got back to her apartment in Clapham Junction.

That night she got out a very small, inexpensive notebook and started making notes. She wrote down all the characters she'd seen on the train. She wrote down details about them. Some of them didn't have names yet. Then she started thinking about Hogwarts and what school life would be like there. She started making a list of the classes the wizards and witches in training would take. She settled on seven as the number of those classes, as well. After this initial burst of creative energy was spent, she went to bed to get ready for work the next day.

It would be another five long years between this creative crush of ideas and the time she finished writing the first Harry Potter novel, seven years from the rush on the train until the first book's publication. In between were long hours of writing during and after work at fairly low-paying jobs and long hours at cafes, making more notes and writing pages of drafts. This cycle continued for several years and still represents the hard work and discipline that continues in Jo Rowling's life today as she progresses through writing all seven of the novels in her vision. Readers waiting for the next novel in the series can take heart knowing that Jo has said she knew on that train ride when Harry appeared to her that the series would be fun for her to write. She enjoys writing the novels and already ponders from time to time the loss that she will feel after finishing the seventh and last book in the series.

What is Jo Rowling's note taking and manuscript writing like? Jo has explained that although the Harry Potter books are works of fiction she had many questions when she met him in her imagination and has spent a lot of time doing what feels to her something akin to research to find the answers to her questions. This notion gives testament to how real Jo Rowling is able to picture Harry's world. For example, she writes notes and biographies on all of the characters just so that she knows their backgrounds. Readers may never read a lot of the background material that she has worked out. She says she needs to know this information herself so that she can understand her characters completely and move them around the page in ways that will be true and accurate to their personalities and what they have experienced in their lives. Ideas come to her all the time, and she uses whatever is at hand to jot them down. She has said that the names of the four houses of Hogwarts, for example, came to her aboard an airplane. She wrote them down quickly on the back of an air sickness bag. Apparently, traveling is a fruitful time for Jo to receive ideas.

In the "Harry Potter and Me" documentary broadcast on the BBC and A&E television networks, Jo showed the audience a representative sampling of scraps from ten years' worth of work on the books. Papers, notebooks, and sketches lay strewn all about her on the floor. She drew the sketches, she said, so that she could see what her characters, such as Harry, the Weasleys, Albus Dumbledore, Hagrid, and others looked like. However, she also sketched the way some things happen in the magical world of Hogwarts. For example, she showed the camera a sketch for the way the bricks in the wall would open onto Diagon Alley that she couldn't find when Chris Columbus, the director of the first film, asked to see how she envisioned that working. The sketch showed a spiraling effect of the bricks giving way rather than the clockwise tap and zigzag of bricks parting open that appears in the film.

Among the papers was a detailed chart listing Harry's first year classmates, complete with symbols that indicate their house at Hogwarts—Gryffindor, Hufflepuff, Ravenclaw, or Slytherin—as well as their parentage, and how magical they are. She says this information is necessary for her to refer to quickly because these matters are important to the allegiances classmates form at the school and to their various responses to the Death Eaters. The chart looked water stained and well used. It's important to Jo that authors know all of the background information on every character because, she says, the author is the one who must move the characters across the page. Readers should have the confidence that the author knows more than they do about each character. In that way they trust the author and enter more fully into the imaginary world of the story.

One detail Jo had to work out was the date when Harry was born. She gave Harry Potter her own birthday, July 31, as a kind of inside joke, she says, because so few famous people she'd heard of shared a birthday with her. She also needed Harry to turn 11 during the summer, so that the invitation letter from Hogwarts would come to him while he was staying with the Dursleys. It is strangely ironic, indeed, to consider that Daniel Radcliffe, the actor who portrays Harry in the first two films, also shares this birthday with Jo and Harry.

Among the other papers and notebooks Jo showed the documentary audience was a Portuguese diary that was not filled in, since Jo says she has never filled in a diary. On the inside cover of the diary, however, are Latin words and phrases with translations, as well as sketches. The work, Jo says, shows her trying out different names for the Dementors. Other papers, sheet after sheet of them, are filled with Jo's handwriting. She wrote on the backs of other papers—one set of notes she showed in the documentary was scribbled on the back of her application for housing benefit (welfare). She writes in longhand (she is right-handed) in notebooks, then types up what she has written on the typewriter or the computer. In the early days, when she didn't own a computer, she typed up notes and manuscript on typewriters at work or at school, even typing up complete duplicates of the first manuscript by hand.

She showed pages of what she said were at least 15 drafts of the first chapter of the first book. The biggest problem she had with the first chapter, she says, was that the chapter kept giving away the whole plot of all seven planned books. Taken together, she relates, all 15 drafts would give away the entire story from the series. At the same time, Jo showed the audience a yellow folder containing a green notebook with a white triangle on the cover with writing inside it, and some loose pages, which Jo said is the epilogue, or last chapter of book seven. She says she wrote the last chapter as a goal to motivate her to finish the writing between where she is now and the end of the series. It was a way of telling herself that she would get there one day, and that when she arrived, the work already done would be there waiting for her. The epilogue, she says, tells what happens to all of the characters after they leave Hogwarts—that is, all of the characters who survive, since Jo relates that there will be more deaths, even of characters who are loved by her and her readers.

While working on the first phases of *Harry Potter,* Jo spent many lunch hours at cafes. Not knowing much about their private coworker, her officemates would often tease her that she must be having a noontime affair. In a way, she was, and her loyalty to her ideas and the world Harry brought to her in her twenties is clear when one considers the kind of social life with young fellow colleagues she was giving up in order to pursue Harry's story.

By the time her mother died, six months after Harry had entered her creative life, and Jo moved to Portugal, she had several pages of notes worked out. Jo admits that the emotional center of book one, the scene with the Mirror of Erised, came about as a direct response to her mother's death. Initially in the writing of the first book, she says, she killed off Harry's parents rather matter-of-factly. Six months later, when her own mother died, she empathized more with how young Harry might have felt at the loss of his parents, and the Mirror of Erised scene, where Harry sees his heart's desire, the sight of both of his parents smiling at him, grew out of that emotional connection between Jo and her character and the loss of her mother. She has said that if she could have spoken with her own mother in such a mirror, she would have told her all about the birth of her daughter, Jessica, the success of her books, and then would have ended their conversation realizing she had never asked the key question of her mother of what it was like to be dead. Like Harry, she would have wanted just five minutes more with her mother alive. Coping with her mother's death has taught her, she says, that there is never enough time. Death, in fact, is a major theme of not only the first book but of all seven, she reveals. When parents ask her about the appropriateness of this theme to children's books, Jo has responded that she is writing the books as she has envisioned them from the beginning, whether children read them or not. They are stories that explore good and evil and include painful and sorrowful deaths, and her purpose is to write about these stark realities as she sees them, not to make anyone's children feel protected.

- By the time she had Jessica in the summer of 1993, Jo says that the work had gone very well, and she had the first three chapters of *Harry Potter and the Philosopher's Stone* written almost exactly as they appear today, as well as a draft of the rest of the book. When Jo and Jessica left Portugal and arrived on her sister Di's doorstep at the end of that year, her notes and manuscript pages for Harry came along with them.

Even though her first husband, Jorge Arantes, claims that Jo shared Harry with him, Jo insists that her sister was the first person to read his story in those dark winter days of 1993 and 1994 when she had moved to Edinburgh after the break-up of her marriage. Jo has often said that if Di hadn't liked Harry at once and laughed and been charmed by his story at a time when Jo was feeling so low about herself and about life in general, she is not sure what Harry's future might have been. By that time, she had already been working on the books for more than three years. But just like she did when Jo told her stories on Nicholls Lane when she and Di were girls playing with the Potters on the street, Di did laugh, did like Harry, and encouraged her sister to carry on.

Although Jo was committed to telling Harry Potter's story, she now had a baby and herself to support and hadn't lost all sense of the practicality that Pete and Anne Rowling had tried to instill in their dreamy daughter. When she discovered that she would need more coursework and student teaching in order to qualify for a certificate to teach French in Edinburgh to support herself and her daughter, she had to surmount the same difficulty that all single mothers with economic challenges face—how to better oneself for the job market while taking care of one's child with a minimum of resources. Jo was a proud woman who knew she needed to get out on her own, no matter how simple her living conditions might have to be. Jo swallowed her pride, applied for government aid, went into counseling, and tried to sort out her life. All this time, she continued to write.

Jo's time in Edinburgh during this period would later fuel the imaginations of mothers and other book buyers everywhere who had heard about her personal journey and were curious to find out what all the fuss was about with this down-and-out-mother and her novel. Jo's small flat at 28 Gardens Crescent, 7 South Lorne Place in the Leith section of Edinburgh has become legendary now, but in 1994 it was a dreary place of survival for herself and her baby daughter, not unlike the confining closet under the stairs where Harry lives when he is with the Dursleys. The second floor apartment had one small bedroom, a tiny kitchen, and living area. It came unfurnished and was anything but cheerful. Nevertheless, it was warm and within walking distance of stores and other places of interest in that area of Edinburgh. Within a mile of her apartment, an area called The Shore was being developed, with bistros and pubs and other facilities to attract visitors and shoppers to the old port area of Edinburgh. However, having lunch at The Shore was not yet as pleasant as it is now, and Jo Rowling couldn't have afforded it then even if it were. Jo says that she did a lot of writing in this apartment, that it was where separate chapters and batches of notes really came together into the first book. At the same time, living there was among the most uncomfortable times of her life.

Jo's well-known method of working in Leith has often been exaggerated to near mythic status. After shopping and feeding, clothing and caring for Jessica, going to counseling, completing paperwork to get into a teacher certification school or secure government aid, visiting with her sister, doing part-time secretarial work, or searching for work that paid enough for her to afford child care and stay at the job, part of Jo's day would involve taking Jessica out for a walk in her stroller. Their normal path was a half-hour walk from their flat to the center of town along Easter Road. If Jessica were not asleep by the time they made it to South Bridge, which she often was, they would walk up Royal Mile, past the many interestingly named shops in the old part of town. The narrow streets and old-time shops, complete with bagpipe music for the tourists, may be reminiscent of Diagon Alley to some Potterites.

Finally, when Jessica fell asleep, Jo would take her to Nicolson's, the coffee shop owned by her brother-in-law, Roger Moore, and his partner, Dougal McBride. She had to climb 20 steps to get to it, but once she and Jessica made the climb, she knew she had a pleasant place to work for as long as Jessica remained asleep. The decor was simple, with many tables with blue and yellow tablecloths and Matisse prints on the walls. She'd slide behind her favorite table in the corner, buy a cup of coffee, position the stroller beside her where she could keep an eye on her daughter, then take out her notebook, and write. Among the numerous tables, she had a favorite window seat that let her look out on the town, and she welcomed both the warmed-up cups of coffee that the staff gave her and the privacy they allowed her. She didn't have to feel guilty about taking up the table, since there were so many available in the cafe. Jo would write, mostly in notebooks in longhand (she is right-handed), hour after hour, for as short or as long a time as Jessica's little biological clock allowed. Perhaps she was comforted by a good omen nearby—one street over from the busy street scene visible from Nicolson's was a road called Potterrow.

One exaggeration about her writing routine in Edinburgh that to this day annoys Jo enough that she has corrected it in interviews is that she went to Nicolson's to write because her flat was unheated or because she couldn't afford to heat it. She says with some indignation that she would not rent a place where there was no heat or where she could not afford to pay the heating bill, because that would obviously put her baby daughter at risk in the winter months in Edinburgh. Still, it is important to note that there are homeless mothers in Scotland, England, America, and many other places, who cannot afford rent of any kind, much less a heated apartment, and must contend with the problem of how to keep their babies warm at night. Even in her most difficult times, Jo Rowling and her daughter were never homeless or destitute to this degree.

In 1995, Jo was able to enter the teacher's certificate program held at Moray House in the middle of the city, sponsored then by the Heriot–Watt

University, now by the University of Edinburgh. Through the generosity of an unnamed benefactor, Jo went off government benefits that summer, and was able to send Jessica to daycare while she finished her coursework full time.

Even during this serious period of retraining for the job market that would secure her and Jessica's economic future, Jo didn't give up working on her Harry Potter novels. They were both her diversion and her lifeblood night after night when she sat home alone with baby Jessica. Sometimes she'd use the typewriters at school to type up her notes between her class assignments. She had no delusions that Harry Potter would save her economically, but she must have known that little Harry Potter was saving her and helping her cope in many other ways. Finally, five years after he'd stepped aboard the train in her imagination as she traveled from Manchester to London in the summer of 1990, Harry Potter was ready to meet the world. Jo could not afford to pay to photocopy her manuscript, so she retyped it completely twice. Finally, she was ready to send it out.

HARRY AND THE OUTSIDE WORLD

Jo sat in Edinburgh's Central Library, leafing through the *Writers' and Artists' Yearbook*. She had already sent the manuscript to one agent in London, but it was rejected, and she was particularly bothered by the fact that they didn't send it back in the special black plastic folder she had mailed it in. She would have to buy another one to package her manuscript in the way she wanted it presented. She tried sending it to a publisher, but it was also rejected there. Looking down the list of agents in the *Yearbook*, she came across the name Christopher Little. She liked his name and jotted down his address.

In February 1996, Bryony Evens was working at the Christopher Little Literary Agency in London. She was a 25-year-old college graduate with an English degree who wanted to break into publishing. She worked in the office. Bryony opened the mail, including the unsolicited manuscripts. When she first opened Jo Rowling's envelope, she took a quick look at the manuscript and dropped it into the rejection pile right away. This was because she saw it as a children's book, and she knew that Christopher Little did not normally represent specialized genres like children's books or poetry.

As part of her normal practice, Bryony checked through the rejection pile again later before she returned the manuscripts with rejection notices. Jo's black plastic folder and hand-drawn illustrations caught her eye, and she began looking at the manuscript more closely. This is particularly unusual, because it is more typical that this kind of special packaging, as well as the author's including her own illustrations, is considered in the publishing world to smack of amateurism. Jo had only sent, however, the standard submission: a synopsis and three sample chapters. This time, Bryony read the whole first chapter and liked it. She set it aside, which meant that the manuscript did not get mailed back with a rejection slip with the others that day.

Bryony mentioned the manuscript to a freelance reader working in the office, Fleur Howle. Surely Fleur and Bryony must be names that Jo Rowling would appreciate, even before she knew what these young women did to keep Harry Potter alive. Fleur read all three sample chapters that Jo had sent in, so she was the first to read chapters two and three. She agreed with Bryony, who then also read the whole submission, that they should ask Christopher Little, their boss, if they could request the rest of the manuscript from this author. Less than intrigued and not having read any of Jo's submission at this point, Chris Little said yes to his assistants' request and went back to his work. Bryony sent the agency's standard letter on Christopher's behalf to Jo Rowling in Edinburgh, asking to see the remainder of the manuscript. There were no guarantees of representation, just an indication of interest.

When Jo got the letter and read it in her dingy apartment, however, she danced around the tiny kitchen table and reread the letter at least seven more times. She mailed off the rest of her 90,000-word novel, *Harry Potter and the Philosopher's Stone*, right away, and it was in the agency office within the week. The manuscript was long by most middle grade (ages nine to twelve) children's novel standards, which are typically in the neighborhood of 40,000 words. Jo explains that she tried to hide this fact by single spacing one version of the manuscript, but had to retype her submission, word by word, double-spaced. Since she could not afford a computer, Jo did this typing at her school, often while Jessica played with jigsaw puzzles at her feet.

Bryony Evens read the book manuscript straight through. After she gave her high endorsement of it to Chris Little, he took it home and read it overnight. He came into work the next day with a few comments that they sent along with others from Bryony to Jo. One comment Bryony had on the early manuscript was that she thought Neville Longbottom could be developed more than he was at that time. Chris Little suggested that Jo make Quidditch a bit more important in the book, since he thought the game would appeal more to boy readers if they could read the rules. Jo had the rules all worked out in her "research," of course, so they were readily available to be put in. Readily available is perhaps a bit of an exaggeration, however, when one considers that Jo had to retype all of the pages that she was changing without the benefit of a computer.

After a few correspondences about these small revisions, Bryony and Chris had a manuscript they were satisfied to show to Little's partner, Patrick Walsh. Walsh also liked the book, and an agreement was made to represent Jo Rowling and take the book to market. They mailed Jo a contract, which she initialed in all the places indicated, and the process began.

Bryony prepared the manuscript at Little's agency and mailed it out to publishers. One of the fascinating aspects of a huge success in publishing is finding out who turned down what would prove to be a golden opportunity. Penguin was the first publisher to reject Jo Rowling's book. Another chance to publish the book was passed by when the woman who would have read it at Transworld was off sick, and the manuscript lay idle in her inbox until Bryony asked for it back to send to another publisher. Finally, HarperCollins was sent a copy, as was Bloomsbury's new children's department. Barry Cunningham of that department called the Little Agency to offer $2,250 (£1,500) to publish Jo's book. Bryony then called HarperCollins, told them about Bloomsbury's bid and asked whether HarperCollins was still interested and cared to bid higher. Harper representatives said they liked the book very much but that they didn't have the time just then to prepare a bid, so they would pass. In all, about twelve publishers declined the manuscript before Bloomsbury bought the rights to publish the first edition.

Jo's share of the sale was about $1,910 (£1,275), after Little's commission was deducted. She received half of it at the sale and would receive the other half at publication. The book moved toward production and was scheduled to come out in the summer of 1997, among over 100,000 books that would be published in Britain that year.

Bloomsbury arranged for Jo to come to London to meet Barry Cunningham and Christopher Little. They met in a brasserie in Soho, near Hamley's toy store, where Jo later popped in and bought something to bring back to Jessica. She made the five-hour train ride to London from Edinburgh and the five hours back again on the same day so she could return to her daughter. It's interesting that Jo bought Jessica a toy with her first advance. She has commented so often that one of the aspects of being so financially strained that hurt her the most was seeing Jessica play with old, smelly, and worn-out toys. Little did Jo Rowling know after her lunch in London with Cunningham and Little that the days when Jessica would have to play with the discarded toys of other children would be very limited indeed.

Bloomsbury's Barry Cunningham has commented on his observations of Jo at that first luncheon. He noticed that she was nervous and somewhat fidgety in a caffeine-driven sort of way. He says that she was less confident about herself but very sure of her story and of its appeal to children. Both Barry and Jo remember Barry's comment to her at the end of their meeting. Realizing that she had had hard times since she returned from Portugal, he told her that she would never make any money in children's books. The statement is one of Jo Rowling's and Barry Cunningham's favorites to relate to others now in hindsight.

Included in the details Bloomsbury needed to work out was Jo's pen name. She had signed the cover letter for her manuscript Joanne Rowling, but the publisher wondered about using this name on the cover of what they saw as a children's book that had marketability to boy readers. They thought that boys might frown on picking up a book by a woman, and they asked Jo whether she wouldn't mind going by her first two initials instead. Thrilled at the imminent publication of her first book, Jo was not fussy about what version of her name appeared on its cover. However, she, like her mother Anne and her sister Dianne, had not been given a middle name at birth. When she thought about a middle initial—perhaps standing for the name of a beloved relative as many people's middle names are—she thought of her late, favored grandmother, Kathleen. She liked the sound of J followed by K as it is in the alphabet. She also liked its similarity to Tolkien's initials J.R.R. She decided to tell Bloomsbury to put those initials on the book, and that is how the pen name of J.K. Rowling was created. As it turned out, having a pen name that is slightly different than her personal name has turned out to be handy for her in the tricky business of keeping her personal and public lives separate. Years later feminists would cry foul and lament that once again a woman had succumbed to the commercial pressures of publishers to sublimate her true identity and disguise her gender, as was the case with George Eliot and many other women in literary history.

While production for the first novel went forward, Jo graduated, earning her teacher's certificate in July 1996, and began looking for teaching work for the fall. She also found out about a Scottish Arts Council grant and applied. Though, technically, her first book was not yet in print, and the grant was for published authors, she did have a contract that publication would occur soon, and she made an argument in her application about her child care costs and financial need and included forty pages of Harry Potter and the Philosopher's Stone with it.

She got the grant, which up until that time was the largest single sum of money Jo Rowling had ever received—$12,000 (£8,000). With this money, Jo bought a computer that would put an end to the retyping of her manuscripts, but not an end to her preference for drafting in longhand. She also used the grant money to provide for herself and Jessica while working to finish the second novel.

Finally, on June 26, 1997, *Harry Potter and the Philosopher's Stone* was published by Bloomsbury in both hard cover and paperback editions. The first printing was only 500 copies. When Jo received her copy, she walked all over Edinburgh holding it under arm. She was thrilled to see it on sale in the bookstore, and swears that Jessica's first words, "Harry Potter," came without any outside prodding from her. There was not a lot of publicity for the novel at the time, but there was a good review in the *Scotsman* and another in the *Sunday Times* that brought some attention. Unfortunately, Barry Cunningham's budget in the children's department at Bloomsbury was so small that he could not bid on the U.S. rights to the book they had just published in England. Even if he had, it is doubtful he would have been able to bid successfully because of what was about to happen next.

Wild About Harry

Three days after the publication of her first novel, Jo Rowling received a phone call from Christopher Little from New York that would soon change her economic status for the rest of her life. There was an auction going on for the international rights to *Philosopher's Stone*, and the bidding for the American rights was going well. Unlike what has been written previously, Arthur A. Levine, Vice President of Scholastic Books and Editorial Director of Arthur A. Levine Books, says that he had been given the galleys for the book by Ruth Logan, Rights Director at Bloomsbury, in March 1997. He read them on the plane back to New York from the Bologna Book Fair. When the bidding reached five figures, Levine had to keep asking himself if it was worth each higher bid that he put on the table. When the bidding went to $100,000, Levine kept going and clinched the purchase with a record-breaking bid of $105,000 for an unknown author's first work of fiction for children.

Levine says he was attracted to the story because of the way Harry had spent the first eleven years of his life not recognized in the muggle world. Harry reminded Levine of the academically or artistically gifted students in public schools in the United States who aren't necessarily as gifted in other, more popular, areas. Levine himself was a musician and remembered how it felt to be among the musicians rather than the star athletes, who are in the mainstream of school and community support. There was little appreciation for Harry's gifts and talents as an individual before his invitation letters to Hogwarts came along. Harry's situation reminded Levine of the underdog, of all people who are marginalized from society in one way or another. He thought that aspect of the story had universal appeal. It is a victory for the reader to find out with Harry that he actually possesses powers no one else around him has. He is a great wizard with a legendary history. He just hadn't known all that about himself before.

When Christopher Little next called Jo to tell her about the sale and to inform her that Arthur Levine would be calling in ten minutes to congratulate her, she says she nearly lost consciousness. She says that Mr. Levine was gracious when he called and told her not to be afraid, which she admitted she was. Among the details to be worked out was Scholastic's concern for the title and a few other words in the British version that they thought might be confusing for American readers. Eventually Scholastic and Jo made some changes for the American audience that became controversial later on. Jo agreed to change the title, for example, from *Harry Potter and the Philosopher's Stone*, as the book was known in Britain, to *Harry Potter and the Sorcerer's Stone* in the United States. She refused to change "mum" to "mom," but she did go along with other changes such as the word "jumper," which means a sweater in England but a girl's dress in the United States.

While all this was going on, Jo had completed book two, *Harry Potter and the Chamber of Secrets*. She submitted it to Bloomsbury two weeks after the first book was published. If there is anything a publisher likes to see, it is a popular first author who has new material to offer right on the heels of her recent success. In this respect, Jo Rowling's plan of a seven-novel series probably fueled the phenomenon at its outset almost as much as Scholastic's record purchase price. Certainly, any lull between novels would have slowed the momentum of the excitement over the series at the start of the craze, just as the lull in 2002 between books four and five was reported by some to have done.

Jo has said the second novel, *Harry Potter and the Chamber of Secrets*, was the most difficult to write because it followed on the heels of the first novel's success. This is frequently the case with successful first novelists. There is a fear that the next book cannot possibly be as good or as popular as the first. Jo had an advantage, however, in that she was still working through the same story lines with the same principal characters and was not introducing an entirely new story to her audience. Harry created his own interest by enticing readers to want to know what would happen to him and his friends next.

Though she turned in the manuscript to Bloomsbury on time while simultaneously teaching part-time, Jo says that she took it back for six weeks to rework aspects she wasn't quite satisfied with. She was happy with the changes, and apparently so were her readers, because when book two was released in the summer of 1998 sales shot the book immediately to number one on bestseller lists.

The story that created the biggest buzz, other than the American sale of the first book, was the myth-making that began about her hard times in Edinburgh. Strangely enough, she and Jessica were still living in the South Lorne Place apartment when some of the stories were printed. Soon, a window was broken and a burglary took place at the apartment. Jo had already survived one previous burglary in Manchester years earlier that had resulted in the loss of meaningful gifts from her mother. She wanted to get out of South Lorne Place as soon as she could find the right house with a good school nearby for Jessica.

With money from the Scholastic sale, Jo moved herself and Jessica to 19 Hazelbank Terrace in Edinburgh. She bought the upstairs apartment in a house, which was in a nice, middle-class neighborhood where children played and some families had lived for thirty years or more. Each of the two-story houses along the street had a little garden in front. Jo was too fidgety to adopt this favorite pastime of Anne's, so she didn't mind that the garden space in front of her house was paved over. Instead, she enjoyed having an office in a converted attic above the living space and was delighted to give five-year-old Jessica her own room for the first time.

When Jessica began primary school at nearby Craiglockhart Primary School, the mothers who waited outside for their children had no idea that the Jo they talked to was the famous J.K. Rowling of Harry Potter fame whose books their children carried to school under their arms. Jo appears to like this separation between her public and private lives, though it becomes a little more difficult to achieve with each new book and film release. Eventually, the neighbors did find out, of course, but it is a testament to Jo's good choice of neighborhood that most treated her with respect and gave her the distance that they would want themselves.

In school, Jessica was young enough at first that her friends were not part of the Harry Potter craze, but the older children soon began pumping Jessica for information about the books to come, even though she had not yet read any of the books at all. To appease them, Jo did a reading at the school in return for the students leaving her daughter alone on the playground. She wanted to wait until Jessica was seven to start reading them to her. In the end, Jo decided to begin reading them to her sooner than she'd planned just so that Jessica would know what all the fuss was about.

Jo says that she was nervous about reading them to her daughter because she wasn't sure what she would do if Jessica didn't like them. Fortunately for them both, Jessica loved the stories.

Now that Jo had secured a comfortable living space for herself and her daughter, pets regained their prominence in her life. Jo acquired a cat she named Chaos, perhaps reflecting her great sense of humor at the cat's behavior but also quite possibly the roller-coaster ride her life had taken in the last several months. It would probably not surprise Jo's mother, Anne, in the least that Jo gave in to Jessica and bought her a rabbit when she asked for one. Jo and Di had both wanted a rabbit so badly when they were girls. Perhaps Jo's parents could enjoy a sweet revenge on Jo, however, when the cuddly dwarf bunny that Jo thought she had bought for little Jessica grew to be a lop-eared giant. Instead of purchasing another rabbit as a companion for the first one and winding up with fifty bunnies to find homes for, Jo bought a guinea pig. One presumes she kept this guinea pig out of the yard, and away from foxes, at night.

In just a few short months, after many long years of struggling, Jo Rowling was able to write full time and care for her daughter, who was enrolled at a good school. She was free to write during the day while Jessica was in school, or to go about town, shopping for food or occasionally stopping in at coffee shops to do a little writing by hand. Life slipped into a comfortable and protected routine for Jo and Jessica at Hazelbank Terrace—at least as routine as life could be for the full-time author of the Harry Potter novels. They had pets, such as Jo's tropical fish, a guinea pig named Jasmine, which had been named before he arrived, and a black rabbit with wild habits that Jessica named Jemima, a name her mother thought to be highly inappropriate. Jo still frequented Nicolson's for a while, but soon left when tourists and other visitors came by to look at her as a curiosity. Eventually, Nicolson's was put up for sale after having been remodeled and made into a more stylish restaurant with an added bar. The remodeling ruined it as a writing place for Jo.

Jo and Jessica remained very close, and their only times apart were during the promotional tours Jo would make for the novels upon their release. In October 1999, Jo made a visit to the United States to promote *Harry Potter and the Prisoner of Azkaban*, and she has described how the tour affected her. She had been to America once before, reading to a respectable audience of about 100 fans. She was not prepared, however, for the change brought about by 1999.

She began the tour in Boston, where she was to do a book signing at a bookstore. She had been reading biographies of the Kennedys at the time and wanted to visit the Kennedy Museum while she was in town. As her car made its way toward the bookshop where she was to appear, she asked Kris, the Scholastic representative who was taking her, if there was a good sale nearby because people were lined up around the block. It was then that she was told that these people were lined up to see her. Jo was floored. The scene became a little like The Beatles' New York City tour of 1964. Jo says she was taken in the back of the store and walked upstairs where she came out in front of an enthusiastic crowd. It was like being a rock star, she says. People were cheering, and camera flashbulbs kept popping and flashing. She didn't know how to compose herself, what attitude she should present to all of these people looking at her and wanting her to sign their books. She tried to look friendly, but all the while she feared she looked guilty for seeing them all there or somehow acted a bit shady about the whole thing. In all, she signed 1,400 books that day.

She did make it to the Kennedy Museum while she was in Boston. On the way, she kept talking to her driver about the Kennedys. It turned out that the driver had once dated Edward Kennedy, the long-time senator from Massachusetts and younger brother of John F. Kennedy and Robert F. Kennedy. Jo stopped the woman from telling her anything more for fear the woman's kiss-and-tell story would affect Jo's high regard for the family.

Jo has been asked what was the most extravagant purchase she made when she got more comfortable with money. She does not point to her house because even though that was probably the most expensive purchase, she feels she was providing a more comfortable living for Jessica. Instead, she describes a low moment when she was writing book four and the paid interview of her former husband had just appeared in the press.

She'd sat at a cafe for two hours, trying to write but finding herself looking at a blank page. The interview was troubling her, not only because Jorge Arantes was taking inappropriate credit for influencing the novels but also for the way he had characterized their marriage. She'd never expected to have her personal life splashed across the papers just because she had published a few books. The words weren't coming; she was stuck on a problem in the book, concerned about the book as a whole, and just generally feeling sorry for herself. Fame was a double-edged sword, she realized; but there was a good side to being put through this, and she needed to feel that good side immediately so that she could get past the bad of the moment. Impulsively, she says, she got up and went to a jewelry store where the week before she had admired a large, square-cut aquamarine ring that was very expensive. She walked in and bought it with no hesitation. She also bought a couple of items for two female friends while she was at it. She says the ring is so large that it's too heavy to wear while she types so it's one of those things she only wears on special occasions and leaves at home most of the time.

Jo's North American promotional tour in 2000 for *Harry Potter and the Goblet of Fire*, book four, was held predominantly in Canada, where she made appearances at major venues to do readings to huge audiences. The reasoning behind this was that Jo could reach more children in a shorter amount of time away from Jessica. Although she concedes that reading in a stadium is not like reading in a small room with only a few people present, she says that the act of reading itself carries with it an intimacy that can reach out and touch listeners, no matter how many are there at the same time. At one event at the Skydome in Toronto, she read to 12,000 fans. Another event was in Vancouver, where she read to almost the same number. The alternative, she says, would have been many events with smaller audiences, which would keep her away from home and Jessica longer, or to have reached a very limited number of children. That year she opted for the stadium route, a method of touring she may or may not change in the future. Additionally, she has participated in several online chats on the internet, which her publishers have set up, and she has appeared on several American television programs such as *The Rosie O'Donnell Show* and *Larry King Live*, as well as given interviews to national magazines such as *Newsweek* and Oprah Winfrey's *O Magazine* in the United States.

Part of the increased hype surrounding the fourth book in the series, *Harry Potter and the Goblet of Fire*, came from Jo's request that it be released on the same day—July 8, 2000—in the English-speaking areas of the world, including England, the United States, and Canada. That meant that British children would not have a heads up on those in North America. Amazon.com took advance orders and offered free overnight express shipping. Bookstores in the United States hosted Harry Potter parties at midnight and had lines of children, some dressed in costume, staying up late during their summer vacation and stretching out the door to buy the first copies for sale after the clock struck twelve.

In England, Bloomsbury had set up an elaborate promotional tour in July 2000, during which Jo would ride a 57-year-old antique steam engine made to look like the Hogwarts Express over a few days across Britain, stopping at stations along the way. A reporter for the Canadian Broadcasting Corporation (CBC) rode with her and interviewed her over three different sessions. During the interviews, Jo kept speaking about the tour itself, obviously feeling badly when she could only wave from her cabin window at all the children who had come to have her sign their books. She indicated that there had been some kind of mix-up, that the press had suggested that she would be getting off at each stop to do book signings, so that is what the fans expected would happen. Instead, the crowds were so huge that security told her to stay on board and wave from the windows. The disappointment on the children's faces, to the point of crying in many instances, was hard for Jo to take as the train chugged out of the station again away from them. This problem, along with the fact that the engine had mechanical troubles resulting in its needing to be towed behind a diesel engine, make it doubtful that Jo will agree to cooperate with that kind of promotional stunt again.

Jo says that, next to writing, answering children's questions about the books is her favorite thing to do. For five years she was the only person on earth to know Harry Potter, and she still enjoys sharing with her audience the intricate details and excitement about the stories. Her readers are becoming more sophisticated as the novels progress. They ask good questions, and some have even pointed out inconsistencies here or there that keep Jo on her toes. Fans have set up websites that list everything from all of the characters' names and progressive histories to allusions from mythology and other sources. Books written about the novels by children and adults alike are hitting bookstores with increasing rapidity. Jo and her publishers are careful to say that none of these projects has been endorsed by Jo.

It is surprising, Jo has said, that her life between promotional tours is fairly normal, despite a few noticeable changes. When *Harry Potter and the Philosopher's Stone* came out, she began receiving fan letters, the first of which was addressed "Dear Sir." The writer received a prompt response from Jo, correcting the mistake. After the novel appeared in America, her mailbag overran her house, and the former secretary turned celebrity author had to hire someone to help manage it. Additionally, Jo hired an American nanny to help with Jessica when her schedule became chaotic. Although she and Jessica continued to live at Hazelbank Terrace for quite some time, Jo would later become a millionaire and buy a Georgian mansion in the well-to-do Merchiston area of the city, another Georgian in Kensington in London, and eventually an even larger residence, Killiechassie House, in Aberfeldy, Perthshire, Scotland, purchased in 2001, at a time when more than she and Jessica would make up her family.

THE NOVELS

Many have tried to understand what it is about the novels that makes them so popular with children, and, particularly after the first film release, with the increasing number of adults who are picking them up and enjoying them as well. That question will take years to answer properly, most likely; certainly it will take writers and scholars of literature and popular culture several years after the publication of the seventh and concluding book in the series to analyze the overall quality and characteristics of the books and the Harry Potter Phenomenon they helped create.

Many analysts are already surprised that children at the turn of the millennium, many of whom have access to more information and more sources of entertainment than anyone before them in history, should still send the message to their adult caretakers that none of the bells and whistles, high-speed games, or technical gadgets replace the value of a storyteller who can spin a good yarn in a way that shows she understands what it's like to be one of them.

Harry Potter is an orphan boy who was deposited on the doorstep of his aunt and uncle, Petunia and Vernon Dursley, at Number 4 Privet Drive, by the great wizard Albus Dumbledore and Professor McGonagall, a teacher at Hogwarts School of Witchcraft and Wizardry. The baby Harry sported a fresh, lightning bolt–shaped scar on his forehead that he had just received in a mysterious ordeal with the villain of the series, Voldemort, who had also just killed his parents. Harry was brought to the Dursleys to live for eleven years as a means of protection. However, the Durleys are muggles, people who do not believe in magic and are not wizards or witches. They treat him badly over the years, making him stay in a closet under the stairs while their own son, Dudley Dursley, spoiled and fat, enjoys all the comforts that the Dursleys can bestow upon him.

The treatment of Harry by the Dursleys is fairly Dickensian to say the least. He is not given any birthday presents and must wear Dudley's old clothes. On his eleventh birthday, however, something magical indeed happens that changes Harry's future forever. He is about to discover who he is, and the rest of the novels continue to let him in on more and more details about his identity and what will become of him, much as children increase in this self-knowledge with each advancing year.

Each of the books so far takes place during one school year at Hogwarts, beginning in the summer just before Harry goes to school and ending with Harry returning to the Dursleys for his summer vacation. Readers wonder why Harry must return to the cruel Dursleys, but there is some indication in the books that it is for his own protection still; however, the details of this are only becoming clearer in the later books.

The principal knowledge that Harry gleans in the first book is that he is a wizard. He never knew this before Hagrid, the gamekeeper at Hogwarts, comes to take him to the school for his first year. Hagrid is a giant with a rough exterior but a very gentle and loving way. Jo once described him to Robbie Coltrane, the actor who portrays him in the first two feature films, as a Hell's Angel motorcyclist who keeps a garden in the back of his house. Hagrid looks after Harry and becomes a trusted friend.

Much of the novels are involved with Harry and his classmates learning how to be proper wizards, with classes in casting different spells with their magic wands and knowing what kinds of potions cure what kinds of conditions and make the desired results come about. On his first train ride to Hogwarts, aboard the Hogwarts Express, Harry meets two friends his age who will stay close to him for the duration of the first four books, at least. One is Ron Weasley, whom Jo has admitted creating from several characteristics of her high school friend, Sean Harris. Ron comes from a large family of redheads and has several older brothers, including a troublesome set of twins, who are already quite acquainted with Hogwarts. He lives with his mother and father, older brothers, and younger sister in a stable and happy home, and there is always a loving commotion going on, with the twins causing mischief of one sort or another. As one of the younger siblings, Ron has seen all of the older ones accomplish achievements of one kind or another before him. His large family is strained financially, to the point where Ron wears mostly ill-fitting hand-me-downs and carries a sandwich made at home by his cheerful and loving but busy mother as an alternative to buying expensive treats on the Hogwarts Express. Coming from such a large family, Ron is looking for a way to make a name for himself. He is fun and resourceful and devoted to Harry, but does become jealous of him to the point where they don't speak to one another in one of the books that has been published so far. Ron's mother, Molly Weasley, sees Harry's great need for nurturing and does all she can to treat him like one of her own sons, even sending him her traditional handmade gift, a sweater, for each Christmas.

It is Mrs. Weasley, in fact, who befriends Harry at Kings Cross Station when she sees that he does not know quite what he is supposed to do to reach Platform 9-3/4. She tells him to push his cart with some confidence toward a wall between platforms 9 and 10. Jo has said that she is attracted to the notion of a fantasy world that is depicted as a separate reality that characters can participate in if they have the knowledge of how to access it. Not surprisingly, visitors to Kings Cross Station will not find a platform 9-3/4. However, they do not find a wall between platforms nine and ten either. The city of London has placed a commemorative sign "9-3/4" on a pole where it is assumed it would be, a rather disappointing spot between television monitors showing electronic schedules for platforms nine and ten. In fact, Jo has revealed since that she misremembered the look of Kings Cross Station entirely when she wrote the platform scene while living in Manchester. Instead, she was visualizing the brick walled arches inside Euston Station, an attractive train station designed by Philip Hardwick in the classical style and built for the London and Birmingham Railway at Euston Grove in 1838.

Harry's other friend is Hermione Granger, who, Jo has admitted, is modeled very much after Jo herself at eleven years of age. Hermione is very bright but insecure. She wants to fit in at her new school, but she instantly puts off most of her classmates by being overzealous in answering every question the teachers ask the class and also giving the right answer to every question. Through the stories and her relationship with Harry and Ron, Hermione is learning to be a better friend and realizing that in addition to book smarts, bravery is a very important attribute to have. Along with Harry, Ron, and Hermione, readers initially don't know just who Harry really is or what he is capable of, or exactly how he got the lightning bolt scar on his forehead, or what his implied special powers mean to his future and the future of the wizard world.

When the three friends and the other first years arrive at Hogwarts in *Harry Potter and the Philosopher's/Sorcerer's Stone*, they enter the Great Hall, where a sorting hat determines which of the four resident houses, named after founders of the school many years ago, each of them will join. Each student puts on the hat, which is a pointy but worn witch's hat, and the hat announces their house. The four houses are distinguished by attributes common to their founders, and members of the houses seem to exhibit these traits, as well, getting along with one another because of the personality traits that they share in common. Gryffindor, for example, is made up of members who are, or seek to be, principally brave and good; Hufflepuffs are hard-working, loyal, and seek justice for all; Ravenclaw members are mentally quick and witty; and Slytherins are willful and desire greatness to the point where they will use any means possible to achieve their goals. It turns out that most of the duels and other head-to-head confrontations between houses center on the houses of Gryffindor and Slytherin, though competitions involve all of the houses at one time or another.

Together, Harry, Ron, and Hermione solve mysteries that arise during each school year they are at Hogwarts. So, not only are they learning about how to be mature witches and wizards using all their powers at full force, but they also work through special problems that happen at Hogwarts each year they are there. These problems seem related in one way or another to the secrets surrounding Harry's special identity as the boy who survived Voldemort's murderous rage the night he killed Harry's parents. The spell he used to kill Lily and James (Jo's father's middle name) Potter

backfired when it came to Harry, leaving Voldemort weakened and diminished in form. He lurks about in every book, trying to gain strength in
power and in body so that he can regain his powerful position and presumably rule the world through evil. Encountering great risk, Harry has
come into contact with Voldemort in various forms and strengths in every
book so far.

One of the most interesting features in the books is the game of Quidditch, which is a bit like a combination of soccer and basketball, played in
the air with players zooming above and down into the stadium on broomsticks. Hogwarts has co-ed teams, one for every house, and the matches
are exciting events for everyone at the school. There are even intra-
school tournaments, where Hogwarts plays other wizard schools in different competitions of skill and daring that may not involve Quidditch at
all. One book portrays a Quidditch World Cup one summer where teams
representing their countries compete; the adults also attend and get as
caught up in the sport as the young people.

Other key student characters in the novels include the main bully stu-
dent, Draco Malfoy, and his two sidekicks, Crabbe and Goyle, and Neville
Longbottom, a mellow and meek character who is also growing and ma-
turing through his participation in the special adventures at Hogwarts.
Cedric Diggory is talented and popular and Cho Chang is a good female
Quidditch player.

The faculty members at Hogwarts are a curious bunch, although there
are good and not-so-good teachers there as at any school *Harry Potter*
readers attend or attended as children. Professor Dumbledore is the headmaster, or principal, and appears to be very powerful in the name of good-
ness. He is Harry's protector and the wise father or grandfather figure in
the first four novels. Professor McGonagall is the deputy headmistress.
She is fair but strict and also looks out for Harry. Professor Snape teaches
potions in a room set up like a chemistry lab, and Professor Trelawney
teaches Divination, a class not necessarily taken seriously by all her students, in a dreamy room with crystal balls and star charts. Interestingly,
the position of teaching the Defense Against the Dark Arts class is chron-
ically open, and, not unlike in many real school districts year after year,
the administration of Hogwarts, principally in the form of Dumbledore,
must scramble around to find a suitable teacher for the position before
school starts. Often, it is this new teacher's arrival that adds the mystery
and suspense that starts off each school year, and therefore each book, on
a newly curious note. One of the various Defense Against the Dark Arts
teachers, Professor Lupin, becomes a popular teacher, but he has an infir-
mity that prevents him from being completely reliable. Jo has said that

Professor Lupin is one of the favorite teachers she created because he is flawed and allows children to see that even well-meaning teachers are not infallible. His disability, for lack of a better term, is reminiscent of Anne Rowling's battle with multiple sclerosis. Another teacher, Gilderoy Lockhart, is a vain author of many best-selling books, which presumably gives Jo an enjoyable outlet for writing about the perils of letting publishing go to one's head.

Like any good fantasies, the Harry Potter novels are filled with strange creatures and animals that hark back to mythology or speak volumes about the animal world that exists alongside the human one by being a little bit different than what readers expect. Ron has a pet rat, and Hermione gets a cat. Both prove to have unusual powers. Owls, such as Harry's Hedwig, take and deliver the mail like carrier pigeons. Almost every student has her/his own owl or other closely related bird that provides this service for them. Dragons come in several different varieties native to specific areas of the world. Unicorns and centaurs walk through the Forbidden Forest outside the Hogwarts grounds, and giant spiders and flying creatures called hippogriffs come out of hiding to move about the school as well.

The mythological references, references to languages and word origins, puzzles, and games, are another aspect of the novels that avid readers enjoy. Readers like discovering things like the Latin word *magus*, which means wizard, combined with animal, produces "Animagus," Jo's made-up word for a wizard or witch who can turn into an animal yet keep his/her magical powers. Durmstrang, one of the two other wizard schools that take part in the Triwizard Tournament, is a pun on the German words *sturm* and *drang*, meaning "storm" and "stress." The words were used to describe a type of nineteenth-century German literature that favored showy displays and rebellion. The school competitors arrive on a ship that stays moored out on the Hogwarts grounds. Composer Richard Wagner wrote an opera called *The Flying Dutchman*, which is about a ship that goes astray, sailing all around the world aimlessly because its captain cursed God in a storm. In Germany, the Nazis were said to enjoy the artists of the *Sturm und Drang* movement, of which Wagner was one, so it is fitting that the Durmstrang school of wizard competitors is a bit shady, to say the least.

Another example of Jo's clever use of allusion is the phoenix. The phoenix, Fawkes, is apparently Dumbledore's pet. A phoenix feather from the same bird is also present inside Harry Potter's and Voldemort's magic wands. In mythology, the phoenix is the symbol of immortality. Since Voldemort wants to live forever and defy death, his, Harry's, and

Dumbledore's relation to the phoenix is certainly something to watch. Fawkes's name is also a play on words. In Britain, November 5 is Guy Fawkes Day. Guy Fawkes was the leader of the so-called Gunpowder Plot to blow up the Parliament in protest of the poor treatment of English Catholics. The rebels planted thirty-six drums of gunpowder underneath the House of Lords before they were found out, and many of the rebels were executed. Today, November 5 is commemorated with bonfires. The name Fawkes for Dumbledore's phoenix relates these two stories through the myth of the phoenix rising from the ashes and living forever.

Jo uses Latin roots in the spells and charms in the Harry Potter books, highlighting how so many of the words in English have Latin roots. She sets a maze as one of the challenges for the Triwizard Tournament, which echoes the Labyrinth of Crete. Her names, which she says she loves to collect, come from maps, dictionaries, acronyms she has made up, foreign words from a wide assortment of languages, literature, history, religion, the saints, gravestones, and words she just likes the sound of together. In short, Jo's imagination is widely heralded in her Harry Potter series, but perhaps less known is the amazing array of allusions that abound on every page for those who care to find and learn about them.

Between the wizards and witches faculty and the animal creatures are other characters with human or humanlike qualities. The muggles are humans with no magical powers. They can intermarry with witches or wizards and produce offspring that could be either magical or muggle. Sometimes a magical person is born from two muggles and vice versa, but these are rare and trace back to unknown ancestors. The house elves, like Dobby, are small humanlike beings with very large eyes who serve as slaves to the magical people. It seems that with every new book readers are introduced to more and different kinds of characters.

One of the features readers enjoy most about the books is Jo's ability to combine fantasy with humor. There is dry commentary in several scenes, and others, though perhaps a bit stereotyped, such as Dudley Dursley's large body and Rita Skeeter's nosey journalistic ploys, have reliable cues in them that have made children laugh for generations. Some observers have eyed Jo's treatment of Rita Skeeter as perhaps a tongue-in-cheek revenge on all the journalists who have bombarded her and challenged her privacy since her books have become such a sensation around the world.

Another popular feature of the books for young readers especially is the food. Jo has commented on how much she enjoyed reading about what the characters in books she read as a child, such as *The Little White Horse* by Elizabeth Goudge, had to eat at feasts and other events. In her Harry Potter books, she includes details about this quite frequently and describes the decorations at such festive occasions as the banquets and Halloween Balls in the Great Hall.

Jo says that someone once told her there is a great deal about money in the novels, and she was surprised at the comment. Yet, when she thought about it, she could see what the observer meant. Ron never has enough money; his brothers are always trying to make more money. Harry has lots of money. Coming from someone who lived, even for a short time, in dire need of money, the talk of money that creeps into the novels should not surprise anyone. In addition, Jo has said that money is definitely a concern to children, perhaps more than adults realize.

Each novel thus far contains a climactic scene in which Harry confronts Voldemort, and the reader wonders just how far Voldemort will get in achieving his goal of regaining his full powers of evil that will challenge Harry's seeming powers for good. This plot, which hinges on Harry's identity and the unraveling of the mysteries that surround it, connects all of the novels together and is the principal force that causes readers to be impatient to see the next new installment in the series. Jo is working from her initial master plan for the seven books, but she is very careful not to reveal much about the future novels, despite the tempting desire to appease the pleading of children whom she can tell love Harry every bit as much as she does. She has warned that the novels become darker as they go along, and that death is a central theme in the series. She has tried to prepare her young readers for the deaths of characters they love. Moreover, she has not given any indication that she will yield and spare the characters that she is planning to kill off. She says their deaths are necessary, and readers will come to know why by the end. Like any good storyteller, Jo likes to keep her readers in suspense.

One of the aspects of writing the novels that is important to Jo is that she wants to complete the series on her own terms and according to the plan she originally set out to accomplish when she started them. She has said that if she can stay true to the story as she originally conceived it and labored so hard in obscurity to work through in great detail—without yielding to pressure from readers, critics, reviewers, or other outside people or events—she will be satisfied with her own work.

While there are no full names of living persons in the books thus far, she has used her grandfathers' first names, Stan and Ernie, and she did make a special point to add the full name of a little girl into book four, *Harry Potter and the Goblet of Fire*. This little girl wanted very much to meet Jo the next time she came to Canada on a promotional tour. Her mother had written Jo a letter about it. The girl's name was Natalie McDonald, and she was dying. Jo wrote back and promised to be sure to meet

Natalie the next time she was there. As it turned out, Natalie died just days before that could happen, and Jo pays tribute to her by putting her name in the fourth book. It is one of the first year's names called out by the sorting hat at the beginning of Harry's fourth school year. The reference appears on page 180 of *Harry Potter and the Goblet of Fire*.

In her A&E *Biography* interview and the one on the BBC in late 2001, Jo held out the yellow folder full of papers that she said contains the last chapter of the last book of the series. She has told people right from the beginning that the last word in the series will be the word *scar*, presumedly a reference to the lightning bolt mark that Harry received from Voldemort the night his parents were killed. Jo has said that she chose the lightning bolt because she needed a simple symbol that also suggested a powerful force. She notified readers through that interview that she does know what is going to happen through all seven books, and she is sticking to her plan. She also cautioned any would-be burglars that the last chapter of the last book is not in her house but locked away in a separate location for safekeeping.

While readers speculate between books as to how the series will end, and the hype dims somewhat before it rebuilds for the release of the next installment as well as the next feature film, audiences remain generally patient with Jo while waiting to find out what is going to happen next. For her part, Jo does not appear to tease readers unnecessarily, but she will refuse to answer questions that come too close to revealing plot lines she does not believe she can reveal without spoiling the story, or she will speak about one generality, such as that there will be more deaths. Jo could talk about the entire story of the series with precise detail, book by book, since it is plotted that carefully in advance, but she won't do that. She's not about to ruin a good story.

By mid-2002, the books in the Harry Potter series had sold 150 million copies worldwide and had been published in approximately 50 languages. Dozens of publishing companies around the world publish the books in their own languages, and many times with different illustrators who pick up the flavor of their culture for the covers. Jo has said one of the most beautiful international versions she has seen is the edition from Japan.

While they wait, her audience rereads the novels they do have. Harry Potter fans go online and talk about the books with other fans in chatrooms and on bulletin boards to try to find out any latest scrap of information or insights they can by studying the intricate timelines and other details of the books that are already out. They form fan clubs, share their own stories, and look up the many allusions to mythology and languages. In short, they do what they will do when the entire series is available a few years from now, but they do it with the excitement of sharing the same passage of time and anticipation as J.K. Rowling herself.

HARRY FOR CHARITY

With the amazing popularity of the first four novels and their strong use of humor, along with Jo's humanitarian interests and personal struggle that have been well publicized in the media, Jo was asked by the Comic Relief organization if she would help them raise money for needy people around the world. Comic Relief was begun in a refugee camp in Safawa, Sudan, Africa in 1985 as a means to raise money for impoverished and abused people in Africa, the United Kingdom, and around the world through the use of humor. Since that time, more than 2,050 professional comedians and entertainers from the United States and elsewhere have donated their time and talents to events such as the annual Red Nose Day to raise money and awareness. Comic Relief has raised over £220 million since its inception. In the United Kingdom, Comic Relief is also involved in helping women who have suffered abuse from the men in their lives. Having worked on injustices in Francophone Africa in her days at Amnesty International and having suffered herself as a mother alone raising her child in less than secure circumstances for a while, the causes of Comic Relief certainly must have struck a chord with Jo.

After she finished book four, which is more than 734 pages long and, according to Jo, pivotal in the series of seven, she took some time away from the seven-book series to write two smaller books especially for sale by Comic Relief. These were samples of Harry Potter's school books at Hogwarts, *Fantastic Beasts and Where to Find Them* and *Quidditch Through the Ages*. Since J.K. Rowling could not have written Harry's textbooks within the setting of the series, these books are authored by the imaginary writers Newt Scamander and Kennilworthy Whisp, respectively. Their real publishers, Bloomsbury and Scholastic, also had to be fictionalized since these books appeared in the wizard world, so *Fantastic Beasts* is published by Obscurus Books and *Quidditch* by Whizzhard Books. Both books appeared in the spring of 2001 and became immediate bestsellers. With everyone involved—from Jo to the publishers to the booksellers putting them on their shelves—forfeiting their share from the profits of the books, more than 80 percent of the purchase price (the other 20 percent covering production costs such as paper and ink) goes directly to Comic Relief.

One of the more interesting features of these companion books to the novels is that they contain some of Jo Rowling's original sketches, which she uses as graffiti. Ron and Harry write one another notes, for example, and Harry makes written comments and doodles in the margins of his reading. Even the books' covers are made to appear worn like textbooks or library books normally appear from frequent use. *Fantastic Beasts* is labeled with Harry Potter's name. *Quidditch Through the Ages* is a popular library book at Hogwarts, so it contains a warning against damage from the Hogwarts librarian and a label showing its history of being checked out by various students at the school. *Fantastic Beasts* is a textbook, so it contains the usual chart inside the front cover where students write their names and the date and proclaim what condition the book is in when they received it.

Readers enjoy the companion books because they are funny and imaginative and also because they provide background about Harry's wizard world in the form of asides to the main action of the stories. Readers learn, for example, in *Quidditch Through the Ages*, that there is an American Quidditch team, though it is just getting started and is not very good because Quidditch is not as popular there. *Fantastic Beasts* outlines and gives readers full descriptions of the various kinds of dragons.

Jo's philanthropic work did not begin and end with Comic Relief. She has also contributed to the Multiple Sclerosis Society in honor of her mother and has made a significant contribution to the National Council for One Parent Families and other organizations that are close to her heart.

In April 2001, Jo opened a resource center for Scotland's MS Society in Aberdeen, a gift valued at $375,000 (£250,000). As a patron of the MS Society, Jo has advocated for more money for research, pain-relieving drugs, and more accessible therapies for MS sufferers. In a moving article she wrote for *Scotland on Sunday*, which was later reprinted in *The Observer*, she told of the disadvantages her mother had in living in the country in Church Cottage. She wrote that in the ten years her mother suffered with the disease in the West Country, she probably saw a physiotherapist fewer than ten times. There was not enough money to bring a therapist all the way to the house, and Anne Rowling could not drive herself to therapy sessions. Eventually, this resulted in her debilitation to the point where she had to crawl upstairs because she could no longer walk. With the proper therapy, this phase of her disease could have been warded off much longer, but Anne Rowling did not receive the help that she needed simply because the therapists could not come that far out. Scotland, Jo wrote, has the largest incidence of MS in the world. Despite this, money for physiotherapy and a helpful drug, beta-interferon, is seriously lacking.

Aside from the huge donations that Jo's books are garnering for Comic Relief, perhaps Jo's largest monetary donation to date is to the National Council of One Parent Families. In September 2000, she gave much-needed publicity to the organization by agreeing to be its ambassador. She has been photographed sitting with children, she and all of them wearing a t-shirt with the organization's logo on the front. Her monetary gift was $750,000 (£500,000). The organization offers help to single mothers with children who are in need. The connection of Jo to this group is obvious to anyone who knows her own history with this problem. A smaller, more local organization that has benefited from Jo's attention and donations is the Maggies Centers in Edinburgh. These centers attempt to bridge the gap in providing counseling and support for cancer patients and their loved ones who might be left in the lurch by hospitals and other agencies. Jo became interested in the centers when she learned that a friend of hers had just been diagnosed with cancer. She has done readings around the country to raise money for new centers to be opened in Dundee and Glasgow.

HARRY AND HOLLYWOOD

Many critics of the Harry Potter series feel that the books' vivid visual imagery and fast-moving plots were conceived for the cinema right from the start. It didn't take long before those involved in movies caught wind of the first novel and began vying for the rights to put Harry Potter on the movie screen. Movie rights involved a clever operation of selling and marketing, as well as dealing with the very protective author of a series of books that was not yet completed. While Christopher Little held out for the best deal, Jo Rowling held out for other reasons—in consideration of herself, her readership, and the fate of her beloved characters. Despite the maneuvering and cajoling that went on, the first film was purchased, cast, produced, and released by November 2001, just a little more than four years after the publication of the first 500 copies of the Bloomsbury edition of *Harry Potter and the Philosopher's Stone*.

Within ten days of publication of the first novel, David Heyman, a contact for Warner Brothers in the United Kingdom, was trying to buy the film rights. It would be a couple of years before Christopher Little and Warner Brothers brokered the final sale of $1 million. It was not the biggest film deal ever made, but it was satisfying to Jo, who kept rights such as final script approval and creative input. What she gave away, some might say, was the Harry Potter trademark, which could be used for products Warner Brothers wished to market to promote the film. Jo Rowling retained some control over the types of products they could make, however, especially in Britain.

Once the deal was made, it was time to locate a director. For a while it was rumored that Steven Spielberg was interested. A recognized genius in film, Spielberg would have brought insights into the making of the film that would have likely made it popular immediately, particularly from a child's point of view. It is not clear why he didn't take the project; some indications suggest that he wanted more cinematic license with the story than Jo was willing to provide. In any case, he eventually moved on to do something else for Warner Brothers instead. Eventually, Christopher Columbus signed a contract to direct the movie on March 27, 2000. His film credits included the very popular *Home Alone* and *Mrs. Doubtfire*, among others. He was willing to work with Jo on accomplishing a cinematic version of her story. Since Jo was already a millionaire by this time, she was more interested in the quality of the movie that was to be produced than she was in how much money it would make. Jo was apparently pleased with Columbus's assignment.

Another of the highly publicized searches was for the little boy who would play Harry Potter. From the publicity leaks and rumors from week to week, it seemed like the casting agents were canvassing the whole of the United Kingdom in search of the right eleven-year-old Harry lookalike who could play the part with the right sort of chemistry. After going through hundreds of possibilities at auditions and casting calls, David Heyman went to the theater one day with a literary agent, Alan Radcliffe. By sheer luck, Alan brought his son along to see the play. When David saw him, he could hardly stay focused on the play because he so clearly saw Daniel Radcliffe, with his shy smile and polite demeanor, as the perfect boy to play Harry Potter. As it turned out, Daniel had already done a little acting and was interested in doing more. He had played the young David Copperfield in the BBC production of that classic Dickens novel.

Indeed, with Daniel, Jo, and Harry all sharing the same birthday of July 31, it would seem as though there were something in the stars that brought the three together. Daniel shares Jo's eyes, downcast at the outside corners, that gives them both a rather sad look. The resemblance was apparently not missed on Jo, who said when she saw his screen test that she thought the moviemakers had found the son she'd never had.

Emma Watson, the girl who was cast to play Hermione, auditioned at a casting call at her school. After the release of the film, there would be debate over how much more attractive many viewers found Emma to be than they had imagined Hermione to look like. Hermione was described in the book as quite plain, with bushy red hair and two front teeth that protruded a bit. Emma's bouncy brown hair and perfect smile caused some devotees of the novels to cry foul, that the filmmakers were playing too much to Hollywood with their heroine. Red-haired Rupert Grint, as many point out, is shorter than how Ron is described, but he is thought by most observers to have the character of Ron down to a science.

Casting the adult roles became like a roll call of the finest in British theater. Since she had always seen him in the role, Jo was delighted to learn that Robbie Coltrane had accepted the part of Hagrid. Other notables included Dame Maggie Smith as Professor McGonagall, Alan Rickman as Professor Snape, Julie Walters as Molly Weasley, and John Cleese as Nearly Headless Nick. When Richard Harris turned down the role of Albus Dumbledore, his granddaughter, who, unlike her grandfather, had read and very much liked the books, raised such a commotion that he relented on her account and took the job. Jo succeeded in seeing her movie cast with all British actors, something she had wanted from the very beginning. With the strength and power Hollywood has in the movie industry, this was a major coup on her part. American actors would most certainly have been brought in if she had not persevered.

While sets were built for many of the scenes, such as the Dursley house, the vision of Hogwarts itself was a composite of many cathedrals and abbeys across England. The principal building used for Hogwarts was Gloucester Cathedral, but other views were taken from Lacock Abbey in Wiltshire, Whitby Abbey, and Durham Cathedral. The front pillars of the Gringots Bank came from the exterior of the Australian High Commission in London. One reason the filmmakers kept changing buildings and views for Hogwarts was to maintain the integrity of the school as an imagined place. It simply wouldn't do to have moviegoers familiar with these locations spotting entire buildings they could pinpoint and losing the suspension of disbelief necessary to enjoy the story.

Since the child actors needed to keep up their studies while they worked, it is interesting to know that neither of the actors who played Harry and Ron had read all the Harry Potter books when they began shooting the scenes for the first film. They were supposed to be done shooting in March 2001, but bad winter conditions extended the time and took them away from school until the shoot ended in July. Chris Columbus reported that working with the three principal child actors went very well, that they soon formed a chemistry together both on and off the set. Since they were children, he says, their hours per day for work were limited, which made filming especially challenging, since they were in so many scenes. Performing was not all that was expected of the three children in terms of the project either. Since all three of the leading actors had signed on to perform in the second film as well, they came back from promoting the movie release in the fall of 2001 and resumed working on *Harry Potter and the Chamber of Secrets*, which had already begun.

Jo has said that she is happy with the way the first film turned out, and she predicted her readers would be as well. Apparently, she was right for the most part because in the United States alone the movie broke all previous box office draws for opening day, grossing $31.3 million, and again for the opening weekend, grossing nearly $100 million. The movie went on to be nominated for three Oscars from the Academy of Motion Picture Arts and Sciences: Best Art Direction, Best Costume, and Best Original Score. At the 74th anniversary of the Oscar awards ceremony held in Hollywood on March 24, 2002, the film, however, did not go on to win any awards. In May, 2002, the video and DVD and DVD-ROM releases of the film appeared in stores. They temporarily filled the void left for Harry Potter fans when the publication date for book five had been pushed back indefinitely. Sales were robust. The DVD version included scenes cut from the original film, with a unique twist. Viewers had to solve puzzles relating to the story in order to capture the philosopher's/sorcerer's stone and open the section where the cut scenes were located. Other special features on the DVD version include a scene featuring Hagrid, Harry, Hermione, and Ron that viewers can replay in approximately eight different languages, including Spanish, German, Hebrew, Greek, and Japanese; and a photo album of major and minor characters from the film that depicts clips of each character throughout the movie. Virtual tours of Hogwarts and the grounds around it complement the opportunity for viewers to purchase their own wands in Diagon Alley and try different flavored Bertie beans by clicking on various pictures. If one purchases a computer version of the DVD, the DVD-ROM, other features incorporating games and the film are available by connecting to the internet.

While Harry Potter never did appear on a fast food kids' meal during 2001 or 2002 as Jo says she worked to prevent, he did, indeed, have several incarnations in the commercial world-tie-ins to films that are well-known to children and adults. Nevertheless, it appears the story itself remains the key appeal for consumers. By the summer of 2002, much of the merchandising in the form of toys, clothing, and school supplies were already marked down on sale tables. That same summer, with the release of book five pushed off indefinitely, the release date for the second Harry Potter movie, November 15, 2002, was still very much anticipated by fans. Also that summer, a change in director was announced for the filming of the third novel, *Harry Potter and the Prisoner of Azkaban*. The new director was Mexican, Alfonso Cuaron, who had adapted another children's book for film, *The Little Princess,* in 1995. Cuaron is known to have an edgier style to his filmmaking that would be perhaps more suitable to the increasing complexity of the novels. It was reported that American Chris Columbus and his family were growing tired of living fulltime in England, but that Columbus would stay involved in the Harry Potter project as producer.

Jo Rowling, in the meantime, enjoyed some time out of the limelight while she continued to work hard on book five. Perhaps armed with the criticism she received in some quarters for what they perceived to be apparent haste in getting out *Harry Potter and the Goblet of Fire,* she was more determined than ever to stay true to her own vision and timing for the next installment of Harry's story.

Chapter 6

CONTROVERSIES AND CRITICISM

As with any success, the popularity of the Harry Potter books has made them a lightning rod for several different controversies. These include the traditional challenges to the books; authenticity and origins (did Jo Rowling steal ideas for Harry Potter from other books she'd read?), charges from certain religious groups that the Harry Potter series endorses devil worship and the occult and should be banned, and, more recently, complaints from literary critics about what they see as the mass-produced quality of her writing. Arguments have been presented on both sides of these issues already, despite not all of the series appearing yet in print.

Even William Shakespeare has not escaped the challenge to the authenticity and origin of his world-famous plays. Some believe that Shakespeare never wrote the plays at all, but that they were written by a variety of other playwrights. Surely, the argument goes, an uneducated son of a glove maker could not have written the beautiful language that is still admired many centuries later. Even if luck struck once for this poet/playwright, he most certainly could not have sustained such consistent quality through sonnet after sonnet and so many dramas—comedies, tragedies, and history plays alike. Despite the challenges to Shakespeare's authenticity over the years, however, most scholars still agree that the body of work attributed to him was indeed written by the same individual, and that individual was the man we know as William Shakespeare.

It often comes as a surprise to students to learn that the origins of most of the stories Shakespeare dramatized in his plays stemmed not from the bard's mind, but that he derived his characters and plots from actual events, legends, and gossip he'd heard about town and in the countryside.

Some of his plays are believed to be drawn from other plays written outside of England. *Hamlet,* for example, may have come from a Danish play. So, Shakespeare also encountered the controversy of authenticity (did he write all of his plays himself?) and the controversy of origin (did he think up all of the ideas for his plays himself?).

Jo Rowling has, so far, been free of the charge of authenticity. As an unknown writer who in the late twentieth century submitted her work to a literary agent over the transom and into the slush pile of unsolicited submissions, her remarkable story of discovery against incredible odds is one that every unknown writer dreams about. Since the discovery of the first Harry Potter novel is well documented and Jo is writing the subsequent books in our own contemporary times and has the plot lines all laid out, most people do not question that she has done, and will continue to do, the writing of the planned seven-book series herself.

Where Rowling does face accusations is in the area of the origin of Harry Potter's story. One American author in particular, Nancy (N.K.) Stouffer, charged that her book, *Legend of Rah and the Muggles,* published in 1984, and the books that follow, published between 1984 and 1988, are the basis for Rowling's series. In 1999, Stouffer received calls from friends and family who noticed several elements in common between her fairly unpopular books and Rowling's wild successes. Stouffer's main character is named Larry Potter, for example, has black wavy hair, and wears round glasses similar to Harry Potter's. Indeed, the sketchy drawings of Larry Potter, primitive by comparison to Mary GrandPre's illustrations for the American editions (which Jo has called her favorites), and even primitive to Jo's own sketches of her character as she worked on him, do show a loose resemblance. Larry Potter's mother's name is Lilly Potter, the same as the more famous Harry Potter's mother, Lily Potter. The muggles (same word) in Stouffer's books are creatures with no hair, who take care of two boy orphans. Muggles in Rowling's books are regular people who are not witches or wizards and are not capable of doing magic.

There was no magic in the Stouffer series in apparently more ways than one. Initial sales were weak. The books enjoyed their largest success following the publicity surrounding Stouffer's threat to take her challenge to the origins of Harry Potter to court. By November 2001, an affiliate of Baltimore-based publisher Ottenheimer Publishers, Inc., reported that its April run of 7,000 reprints of Stouffer's books had yet to sell out. Publicity and money, of course, are pointed out as a motive behind Stouffer's action by those arguing in Rowling's defense. Jo refused to end the matter by paying Stouffer off with a cash settlement, even though many said that would be the easiest way for this wealthy author to handle this challenge to her integrity. Most observers believed it was simply a matter of principle with Jo. Not one to hide many of the influences on, and sources of, names and other elements of her work, Jo claimed that her muggles did not come from Stouffer's, for example, but from a name she heard people call one another—"mugs."

On the other hand, it cannot be easy to make a claim such as Stouffer's against a giant publishing conglomerate like Scholastic when the monetary figures are so astronomical and the odds of a fair hearing in the eyes of the public were so unlikely. Stouffer remained a thorn in Rowling's otherwise rosy success. When settlement talks failed, Scholastic, Rowling, and Time Warner Entertainment Company, which owns the film rights to the first two Harry Potter films, filed a lawsuit asking a judge to find that Rowling does not violate Stouffer's copyright and trademark in using the word "muggles," in particular. Stouffer filed a countersuit in March 2000 alleging trademark and copyright infringement. In 2002, the judge found in favor of Rowling, and the case was closed. Stouffer says she has moved from Camp Hill, Pennsylvania, to another rural area of the state because of pressures from the suit and threats she claims to have endured, such as being shot at and receiving a hornets' nest in the mail.

Other books have struck readers as suspicious precursors to Rowling's, even if their authors are not calling foul themselves. One of these is American author Jane Yolen's *Wizard's Hall*, published in 1991. In this middle-grade fantasy novel, eleven-year-old Henry is sent to wizarding boarding school at Wizard's Hall where wizards in training wear scholar's robes and take classes such as Spelling (the casting of spells). Harry Potter is also eleven when he gets picked up by Hagrid to go to the boarding school of Witchcraft and Wizardry, Hogwarts. In Yolen's book, Henry does not think he has any special talent for wizardry, but he is willing to try in order to please his mother. In Rowling's first book, Harry Potter does not know he is already a wizard and accepts Hogwarts as a welcome escape from his miserable life at the Dursleys.

As it turns out, Henry's arrival at Wizard Hall in Yolen's novel has been much anticipated, since he is the 113th student, and, according to a spell, the school needs 113 people to fight off a curse put on it by the master of the dark arts. Likewise, Harry Potter's arrival is much heralded, since he is famous as the boy who survived the treachery of the dark villain Voldemort. Henry in Yolen's novel keeps thinking of his dear ma and things she would say to him and what she might think of his deeds at Wizard Hall. Harry Potter sees a vision of his dead parents in a magical mirror and his love and longing for them is the emotional center of the story.

In *Wizard Hall*, Henry's name is changed to Thornmallow, and on Thornmallow's bedroom ceiling appears a sky of twinkling constellations that periodically light up and call out their constellation names. In Hogwarts' Great Hall, the ceiling appears to be open to the night sky, showing the stars. People move inside of the pictures on the wall at both Wizard Hall and Hogwarts. Another similarity in setting and plot is the Great Hall, which is where the faculty of both Wizard Hall and Hogwarts School of Witchcraft and Wizardry address the student body and strange things happen, including the arrival of mysterious visitors and faculty who appear in different forms, for all to witness with astonishment. As it turns out, Thornmallow, with the help of his friends Tansy, Gorse, and Will, go to the library to look up information on how to beat the Quilted Beast, which is the agent of the master of dark arts. Thornmallow becomes the hero of the school by using a combination of courage, friendship, intellectual prowess, and quick thinking. At Hogwarts, Harry becomes the hero by using the same qualities in various situations, including plotting solutions to problems with his friends Ron and Hermione and making several late night trips to the library to look up information and spells. The overall combination of wizard fantasy and school story in both novels has made comparisons of some of the finer features particularly intriguing for some readers.

If one wonders why no suit has been brought against Rowling concerning this book, it might be because Yolen has accepted the coincidence of authors thinking up similar stories. It does happen. Additionally, "borrowing," just as Shakespeare did with the plots and characters of his plays, is a recognized part of the writing trade. It is interesting to note that unlike the unknown writer Nancy Stouffer, the author of *Wizard's Hall*, Jane Yolen, is a well-known and successful American children's author who has published more than 200 books with well-respected publishers in a long and enduring career. It is also worth noting that some of her books, though not *Wizard's Hall*, have been published by Rowling's American publisher, Scholastic.

Comparisons among readers of a genre such as fantasy, for example, will inevitably bring up suspicions of borrowing among authors and books. For example, Rowling's Platform 9 3/4 at King's Cross Station in London— the gateway to the wizard world and Hogwarts that Harry Potter and the Weasleys reach by pushing their carts through a solid wall—draws comparisons to Eva Ibbotson's novel *The Secret of Platform 13*, which is also located at King's Cross in London above a fantasy world that exists unnoticed beneath it. Despite comparisons like this and others that readers will undoubtedly make and similarities they think they see among works of fantasy, pure coincidence and unintentional, forgetful borrowing are at least equally possible explanations for these similarities as are tongue-in-cheek allusion, artistic pun, respectful nods, or the outright lifting of ideas. Various authors, even those among the most favorite over many years, admit to using these methods from time to time, reworking the sources of their inspiration the way they feel will tell a good story. Readers are left to assume that only the authors themselves and their lawyers can work out any perceived infringements of each other's rights.

Another charge that Jo Rowling has had to deal with, both in person and by reputation, is one that bothers her the most because it concerns the relationship between her books and her readers. That is the charge that the Harry Potter books endorse witchcraft, the occult, and devil worship and ought to be banned, particularly from access to child readers. Harry Potter books have not only been banned from classrooms and school libraries by some public school districts and private schools in the United States, but Harry Potter book burnings have also taken place in the United States, a country that claims free speech as a fundamental right of its citizens.

Some opponents fear that the power of the popularity and hype fueling the Harry Potter craze creates a loss of choice, amounting almost to brainwashing, on the part of child readers. They believe that it is the "Harry Potter Phenomenon," not the books, that kids are responding to. In short, their objection is not to the books, the characters, or the plots as much as to the pressure the phenomenon surrounding them puts on children to "sign up" as a Harry fan or risk life as an outcast at school and on the playground. When teachers join classmates in exerting this pressure to "like Harry," they argue, children who choose not to read the books or cannot read at the level the books demand, especially as the books progress in length and mature in theme, suffer in a way that they should not have to suffer. To help de-emphasize the influence of Harry over children, some adults have engaged in a countercampaign against Harry's "power." These people favor, at least in theory, although some have actually been caught, slipping Harry Potter books off the shelves in public libraries, with the full intention of destroying them.

This kind of censorship becomes institutionalized when school districts formally ban the books from their school libraries. The Harry Potter books have been burned in such places as New Mexico and Pennsylvania and challenged in many other states and in countries around the world. There is a long list of books that have been banned over the years in the United States, many of which have gone on to become masterpieces of world literature. Mark Twain's *Huckleberry Finn* is a classic example. The reasons behind book bannings usually reveal more about the people doing the banning and what they are afraid of than they do about the books themselves. It is interesting that *Huckleberry Finn*, for example, used to be banned in some American schools because of its use of dialect and portrayal of a black man, Jim, befriending a white boy. The fear then, apparently, was the integration of black and white societies. Today, the book is still banned in some places because the novel contains one word that is regarded as highly offensive by today's standards, and the fear is of offending readers, minority group readers in particular. Teachers and critics argue over the use of the word in the context of the entire novel, trying to determine whether or not it is used offensively. Many, including several black literary critics, argue that it is not, and that Twain did more for black and white race relations in America than any other author before him. Others argue against including *Huckleberry Finn* at any level before college because they doubt the sophistication of young adult and child readers to catch the nuances and context of this kind of period speech. The book is not being used in many college classrooms much for the same reason of not wanting to offend readers with the heavily charged "n-word." The argument goes on, more than one hundred years after the book's publication.

Besides fear of mass hysteria or brainwashing brought on by something that is wildly popular in a world heavily influenced by popular culture, Harry Potter book banners are afraid of witchcraft, the devil, and cult behavior. One of the more publicized public burnings of the Harry Potter books happened in New Mexico, in December of 2001, during the holiday season which just happened to coincide with the first theater release of the first film, and just days after Rowling's second wedding. Jack Brock, founder and pastor of Alamogordo, New Mexico's Christ Community Church, led his congregation in a burning of the books. Participants sang "Amazing Grace" as they threw copies of Harry Potter books into the fire. Traces of this fear in American history go all the way back to the days of the Salem witch trials in Massachusetts. Any woman who acted a bit peculiarly in those days was at risk of being charged with witchcraft. She could be hanged for it, if convicted, usually in a mock trial. A related fear and hunting down of suspects on little evidence fueled the McCarthy era of the 1950s, when artists, writers, and others were "blacklisted," rounded up, and charged with being communists.

The people who ban Harry Potter on this basis hear that the main character is a wizard and that the children in the books are going to school to learn to be witches and wizards. They hear that there is a Defense Against the Dark Arts teacher at this school, and the children are encouraged to model the behavior of the wizards and witches on the faculty and not necessarily that of muggles—many of whom are their parents or other relatives—who are not involved in witchcraft and wizardry. They argue that a life with magic is portrayed as superior to the life without it, a source of encouragement of cults among young people.

Many of those who argue against book banning in general, including the Harry Potter books, say that most of those who march against and burn books and oppose the reading of them have not actually read the very books they are protesting against. Otherwise, they argue, these protesters would know that the details they mention are taken out of context in the novels and used for their own purposes. The protesters, the argument goes on, use the very mass hysteria they attempt to assuage by banning the books to incite hysterical overreactions to the material the books contain. Free speech advocates argue that banning a book almost always results in a backlash that is greater than the protesters' original action. The publicity of a book banning or burning only gives the book more attention and raises the curiosity of would-be readers, especially young people, to read it as soon as possible.

For her part, Jo Rowling has acknowledged publicly that she does not believe in witchcraft or magic and is not a believer of the Wicca religion. She has admitted to believing in God. She says that her novels are about good fighting evil, a very basic human struggle that is real and continues to go on in any age or time. What's more, the students at Hogwarts go home for Christmas, a Christian holiday, and other days such as Easter are mentioned in the novels. She argues that children are capable and sophisticated enough to see where the heart of the novels is, that any thought of the books' attempting to sign them up for an occultist group is laughable, and that the children and her other readers know it.

Still, while some conservative Christian groups, for example, continue to make their case on hearsay alone, without reading the novels, others have read the books and make a more thoughtful and structured argument in reply to their Christian counterparts. Connie Neal, for example, in *What's a Christian to Do with Harry Potter?* makes an argument in favor of the moral values in the books and why they do not conflict with traditional Christian teaching.

Groups such as Muggles for Harry Potter in the United States and elsewhere are active in raising awareness, educating the public, and otherwise working to discourage the practice of banning the books. Muggles for Harry Potter is supported by the American Booksellers Foundation for Free Expression, the Association of American Publishers, the Association of Booksellers for Children, and People for the American Way Foundation.

More recently, especially after the release of the first film, there has been a backlash among the literary community against the Harry Potter novels and Jo Rowling's success. At first, professionals who work with children, such as teachers and librarians, enjoyed the fervor surrounding the books as much as anyone. These groups saw their students and patrons reading at record rates; many children were now reading who had not cared to pick up a book before. The magic in Harry Potter, according to many of these professionals, was that the series was encouraging kids to read.

After the movie release, however, and its accompanying hype, promotion campaign, and especially its heavy merchandising, some children's literature professionals and literary critics started looking at the books in a more analytical light. They argued that there was a formulaic quality to the books in setting and in time, and that, similar to television programs, the plots of each book were neatly wrapped up in almost the same ways. Harry is miserable at the Dursleys in the summer. Harry gets to the Hogwarts Express somehow and the school year begins. There is a new Defense Against the Dark Arts teacher and some kind of structured challenge, such as a Quidditch match or tournament, that will test Harry's abilities. Plus there is something strange going on that Harry, Ron, and Hermione have to investigate on their own and otherwise deduce from evidence they can find about what it is and how to survive its dangers before the end of the novel, which will also be end of the school year. Small details about the overarching plot of Harry's true identity and the origin of his powers and whether or not he will be able to save the world from Voldemort are dropped every so often to keep readers turning from page to page and book to book.

Not only do some critics see the plots as formulaic, but there are also charges of sexism, even though Hermione can be argued to be a strong, female character. Many of the females, critics argue, are presented in a negative, or less than strong, light, or, at the very least, female characters such as Mrs. Weasley are nothing more than stereotypes. Jo seems to be obsessed, they point out, with deriding overweight people of both genders in the novels as well.

Another charge leveled at Jo is that her writing style is flat and repetitive and is often in need of better editing, such as in the lengthy book four, *The Goblet of Fire*. There is a growing consensus in the literary community that Jo is sacrificing quality and longevity for quantity and speed.

Many concerned parents, teachers, and librarians are quick to point out that as the themes mature in the remaining novels, as Jo has indicated they will, they may be too troubling for younger readers, who will be enticed to move on in the series by hype, perhaps before they are ready. Popularity is often a suspicious commodity to academics and scholars in the children's literature community; thus, the wild popularity of the Harry Potter series both baffles and fascinates people who study literature and culture and causes a knee-jerk reaction that something must be wrong with the books since so many children take to them so quickly, like fast food. Fast food is not nutritious, they argue, and express a mounting concern that Harry Potter is and will remain fast food for the reluctant reader without much nutrition for the nurture of young minds.

Jo herself has not said that she has written the books as deep artistic expressions of her soul, or argued that they stand up to the best of world literature. She has said she has written the books for herself—with humor, adventure, allusions to mythology and language, and a strong plot of good against evil. These are the kinds of books she likes to read. Additionally, she says she has written a story of what it's like to grow up, since she especially remembers what it felt like to be eleven years old and go through the unsettling time of adolescence.

Other critics and children's literature professionals agree, saying that millions of kids can't be wrong. Reluctant readers are reading the books, they say, because they are readable and because they are really good stories. In an age when most kids would prefer to sit in front of a screen playing video or computer games or watching television, the Harry Potter books are a small miracle in that they awaken children to the power of their own imaginations, which have been dulled by myriad visual images blasting out at them on a continual basis.

The film releases have been met with skepticism among Jo Rowling's critics, even those who would defend her otherwise. They say they take away from the good that the books were doing for children by encouraging them to use their imagination as they read them. A girl who leaves the movie of *Harry Potter and the Philosopher's/Sorcerer's Stone* or the upcoming *Harry Potter and the Chamber of Secrets* film and says that she must have been wrong because she thought Hermione would not be so pretty is a girl who has had her reading experience altered. Some argue that this alteration will affect her future reading and her trust in her own ability to imagine what she reads.

Various "translations" of the novels also mystify some critics, especially what they argue is the "dumbing down" or Americanizing of the British version of the novels. Edward Olson tabulates a count of these, which is published on the "Harry Potter Lexicon" website, edited and maintained by librarian Steve Vander Ark. By Olson's count, over 80 variations of this sort exist between the British and American publications of the first novel; less than 60 in the second; less than 20 in the third; and less than 30 variations occur in book four. If the author and her editors really respected children, critics argue, then they would respect children's ability to decipher a new use of a word that they are unfamiliar with from its context. Perhaps the changes in "translation" from British to American English have slowed down in response to this criticism from American educators.

Still another controversy arose that Jo Rowling had very little to do with, except, perhaps, as a victim of her own success. The *New York Times* decided that the Harry Potter books' places in the top four spots of their well-respected best-seller list for so many weeks unfairly skewed the list in favor of children's literature. They decided to create a separate list for children's books and put the Harry Potter books there. Those who disagree say that, first, Jo has never said she set out to write children's books, and the books have clearly had appeal for adults. Second, the *New York Times*, in their view, has shown a bias against children's literature by segregating it from their mainstream list. If the Harry Potter books are the best-selling books in the country, they argue, readers of both children's and adult's fiction should note that fact.

For her part, Jo has said that when she is approached by parents who say their five- or six-year-old loves the books, she is wary of the wisdom in having children that young begin reading or listening to them. It depends on the child, she says, but she would recommend waiting until a child is at least seven to begin reading the series. Most teachers and librarians see children aged eight to nine and up, or what is frequently called the middle-grade group of ages nine to twelve, enjoying the books with more frequency. More recently, Scholastic has printed paperbacks of all four novels with covers that could be considered more adult in flavor, obviously to appeal to the parents and older siblings of the target reading group. As the novels progress in sophistication and maturity as Harry advances toward adulthood, to which Jo has alluded, it is probable that even more adults will come to read the books. *The New York Times*, and publishers as well, will be confronted with how to classify these later novels in the series, just as they are now having difficulty classifying many titles already in print from other authors and publishers that seem to cross over or bridge children's and adults' categories.

There is no doubt that as a character whose first name his author liked and would have named her own son, and whose last name his author liked and reminded her of good times as a child, the figure of Harry Potter has a future yet untold in more ways than one. Not only are all of his novels not yet published, but his fate as a character in world literature who caused quite a stir at the turn of the millennium is also yet unknown and will remain that way for years to come.

Chapter 7

CONCLUSION

In 2001—the year *Fantastic Beasts and Where to Find Them* and *Quidditch Through the Ages* came out to benefit Comic Relief and the first film, *Harry Potter and the Sorcerer's Stone*, was released—Paul Gagne won the Carnegie Medal for *Antarctic Antics*; the Newbery Medal went to Richard Peck for *A Year Down Yonder*. President George W. Bush took the oath of office after winning one of the closest presidential elections in U.S. history, while they still counted the votes down in Florida. Oklahoma City bomber Timothy McVeigh was executed, and terrorists attacked the United States and the global community at the World Trade Center, Pentagon, and on a fourth hijacked plane over Pennsylvania. At the encouragement of Prime Minister Tony Blair, Britain joined forces with the United States to fight the Taliban in Afghanistan. In Hollywood that year, *Gladiator* won the Oscar for Best Picture. In popular music, Paul McCartney led the Concert for New York City at Madison Square Garden in October for an invited audience of World Trade Center firefighters, police officers, and rescue workers. The concert highlighted many British and American performers that crossed generations in a way both Harry Potter readers and their parents would enjoy. A few weeks later, George Harrison died after a long battle with cancer, leaving only two Beatles, Paul and Ringo, still alive.

When the film *Harry Potter and the Sorcerer's Stone* was released in the United States in November 2001, many American children were taken to see it on field trips from school. While that notion caused problems for some parents and educators, others argued that the children needed this pleasant experience together as one way to help recover from the traumatic events of September 11, 2001. Children in classrooms with a view of the World Trade Center who witnessed the horror of that day especially enjoyed the chance to go with their classmates for a shared happy event in the city, according to some of their teachers. Other children across the country went to see the film with family members and friends, as perhaps the first enjoyable communal outing they'd had since many in the country retreated to their homes for weeks following the terrorist attacks.

In the spring of 2002, Harry Potter fans who had read all the books and seen the movie version of the first book multiple times eagerly anticipated the publication of the fifth novel, reported to have the tentative title, *Harry Potter and the Order of the Phoenix*. In online interviews, Jo has revealed that of all the magical creatures she's created in Harry's world, the phoenix is the one she would most like to have herself. Both Harry's magic wand and the villain Voldemort's contain a feather from the same phoenix, and Albus Dumbledore, the beloved headmaster of Hogwarts and Harry's principal protector, has a phoenix living in his office. While long-time fans can only speculate and imagine where the story will go next, only Jo Rowling, who planned out the major plotlines years ago and has already written the final chapter of the final book with the word "scar" as the final word, knows what will happen for sure.

As Jo continues to work on the series, her personal life seems to have taken a positive turn as well. On Boxing Day, December 26, 2001, at age 36, she married Dr. Neil Murray, age 30, at Killiechassie House, the country home Jo had just purchased with Neil in Aberfeldy, Perthshire, in Scotland earlier that fall. The ceremony was reported to be small, with just fifteen people including her father, Peter; and her stepmother, Janet, who came to Scotland from Chepstow, Monmouthshire; and Neil's father, Ernest, 57, and his mother Barbara, 54, who came to the ceremony from Huntley, Aberdeenshire. The wedding party included Jo's daughter by her first marriage, Jessica, age 8; Jo's sister, Di, age 33; and Neil's sister, Lorna—all serving as bridesmaids. At the brief 20-minute ceremony, Jo reportedly wore a cream outfit, custom designed for her. Dr. Murray was working as a senior house officer in anaesthetics at an Edinburgh hospital when he met Jo about a year before, but he then went on to study for a general practice. This is also Neil's second marriage. He had married his school sweetheart, Fiona, 29, four years before, but the couple subsequently divorced. It was reported that, because of Neil's studies, he and Jo did not take a honeymoon right after the wedding. Jo's family now includes a new husband, a daughter entering adolescence, ever-present pets and as of 2002, a new baby on the way.

Jo Rowling's struggle to maintain a normal private life amid a world of celebrity has been, and will continue to be, a constant challenge. She and Neil, for example, had originally wanted to marry in July 2001, during a planned trip to the Galapagos Islands off the coast of Equador. News of their plans leaked out, however, so they diverted their holiday to the tropical island of Mauritius in the Indian Ocean and postponed the wedding. In order to keep their next wedding plan secret so that they could have the kind of ceremony they both wanted, they hired catering and other services from Edinburgh, Scotland, fifty miles away from the site of the wedding at Killiechassie House. Members of the wedding party were urged not to whisper a word about the ceremony to anyone. As a woman who is among the world's most successful authors, a woman who once dreamed of a rebellious counterculture lifestyle while smoking cigarettes with Sean Harris under the Severn Bridge in Chepstow but who now mingles with royalty and rock stars, Jo Rowling may be only beginning to appreciate the cost of this high level of success.

Jo has met the Queen of England and received an honorary doctorate from both Dartmouth College in the United States as well as Exeter University in England, her alma mater. Jo met Queen Elizabeth II on a visit to Bloomsbury's offices in Soho Square in London. The queen spoke to her about her own love of reading as a child, and she agreed to have her picture taken with Jo. In the background behind them are shelves of Harry Potter books. Later Jo would receive the Order of the British Empire, or OBE award, from Prince Charles, who, as the father with the late Princess Diana of a boy named Prince Harry, has said he is a Harry Potter fan. The ceremony to bestow the award was planned earlier for Queen Elizabeth II to give it to the author, and there is some mystery as to why Jo apparently could not attend at that time. One version has her being ill; another says that she was terrified or that her daughter was ill; still another says that the event conflicted with an event Jessica had at school. Some observers might wonder if there isn't a bit of the Jessica Mitford rebellious spirit still left in Jo Rowling at times like these. There is a well-known photograph of Jo holding the OBE award, a cross dangling from a pink ribbon, in her madeover look as a millionaire—cream suit, blonde hair, pearls, and a tasteful touch of makeup. Some predict that with the release of the second film and fifth book, she may become the first billionaire author in history. She already out-earned the queen in 2001 as having the highest income of any female for that year in Britain.

The invitation to come to Exeter to receive an honorary doctorate degree came at about the same time as the release of *Harry Potter and the Goblet of Fire*, the fourth book in the series. The book, which was facing criticism for being so long, already had begun to challenge its label as a work for children—where so many in her audience had tried to place Jo's work.

The prepublication sales for the book on Amazon.com were 290,000 copies, and the British order was for more than a million. By comparison, a children's book that is selling well might sell as many as 20,000 copies. While the length of book four became intimidating for some readers, others read straight through without stopping. Jo has said that book seven will probably be as long if not longer, because in it she will have to say good-bye.

Jo prepared her honorary doctorate commencement speech for Exeter and took her place in the procession through the Great Hall at graduation ceremonies, the same place where Glenda Jackson had earned an honorary doctorate the year Jo had graduated over a decade before. Among the graduates of the year 2000 was Peter Phillips, son of the Princess Royal, who had earned a B.S. degree in exercise and sports sciences. Jo wore the red and blue robe and cap customary for someone receiving this degree at Exeter and was concerned that the cap was way too large for her head and might slip down or fall off. She was reportedly very nervous about giving her speech. Perhaps she had mixed feelings about receiving the degree and speaking to faculty, students, and parents when she had once been one among them.

Dr. Peter Wiseman, professor of classics, warmed up the crowd with a few humorous quotes from Jo's books, then introduced her. His amusing comments seemed to calm her a bit, as laughter always has. When she got up to give her speech, the students who were there later reported it was the best speech they'd ever heard.

She spoke about the mistakes she had made in her life, how she had not been afraid to take risks, and how a little bit of luck can be a good thing for anyone. She elaborated a bit on each of these themes. She admitted that after she left Exeter she really wasn't sure what she was going to do, although she knew the only thing she really wanted to do was write. She said she was afraid that she would be a complete failure at whatever she attempted, and that this appeared to be playing itself out as she went from job to job for a while.

It wasn't until she really became down and out as a single mother with a child and no marketable skill to bring herself out of poverty that she realized she had nothing more to lose. She could try writing that novel because things could not possibly get much worse than they were already, and she could go back to teaching or secretarial work if the risk became too great. She said she was much happier living with fewer means and writing than she would have been in a financially secure corporate position doing work that she loathed.

Luck also played a factor in turning things around for her, however, she admitted that day to the audience of hopeful graduates. Ever conscious of the unfortunate, she reminded the graduates of how lucky she and they were to have been able to receive an education at that institution when other young people were starving or had no hope for such an opportunity to better themselves. With this privilege, she implied, came a responsibility to use what they were given to help those less fortunate in whatever discipline they chose to work.

Jo's parting advice was to urge the new graduates not to be afraid to risk failure, to follow their dreams. She advised them to know what their own expectations for themselves were and to strive to live up to no one's expectations for them but their own. Finding a life's work to which you could give your all is important, and she advised the graduates to find that work and do it with passion. With that, she said, they should try to live the best and fullest lives possible.

Taking her own advice from the commencement speech, Jo continues to believe that her family and her audience of readers are the only groups of people to whom she owes her loyalty, despite her level of fame. She says that keeping this thought in mind keeps her grounded and at work. She knows that the fame and fortune of Harry Potter is unlikely ever to come again. She believes that she will always write, even after the seventh Harry Potter book is complete, but she has said she is uncertain what her next subject will be. Jo states that she has a file cabinet full of ideas for other works, speculating only jokingly that perhaps next she will write about a Medieval monk. As Harry's fans grow older with her, they will undoubtedly follow her career and take interest in the well-being of Harry's imaginative creator for some time to come.

With her penchant for names, the serialization of her novels, and her popularity with the everyday reader, Jo Rowling is a bit like a modern-day Charles Dickens. With the worldwide excitement over her creation, its appeal to young people, the unpredictability of what will happen next, the success and suspicion of quality that that kind of success brings, and the rock group–like meteoric rise to fame, Jo Rowling's experience has been a bit like The Beatles.

Like fantasy always does, the Harry Potter story takes readers and movie goers out of reality for a while and transports them to a new world via the gift of their imaginations. As a child of the 1960s who enjoyed an idyllic youth on Nicholls Lane in Winterbourne, a bored and challenged adolescence outside the mystical Forest of Dean, and an unsettled young adulthood shuffling from job to job and place to place; as a single mother, facing self-disappointment while at the same time rejoicing in the closeness of her daughter; as a new teacher who'd rather be home writing than doing anything else; as a successful author, and then a worldwide celebrity—as the woman who has lived through all these times and become all these things, Jo Rowling is a survivor who is only just getting started.

APPENDIXES

APPENDIX A   J. K. ROWLING TIMELINE

1964   Anne Volant and Pete Rowling meet aboard a nine-hour train from King's Cross Station to Arbroath, Scotland.

1965   March 14—Anne Volant and Peter James Rowling marry at All Saints Parish Church in Tufnell Park, north of London.

The Rowlings move to a house at 109 Sundridge Park in Yate. July 31—Joanne Rowling is born to Anne Volant Rowling and Peter James Rowling at Cottage Hospital at 240 Station Road in Yate.

1967   June 18—Dianne Rowling, Joanne's sister, is born at home in Yate. The day of her birth is Joanne's earliest memory.

The Rowlings move to 35 Nicholls Lane, Winterbourne. The Potters, Ruth and Graham and their children, Ian and Vikki, lived at 29 Nicholls Lane.

1970   September—Jo Rowling starts primary school at St. Michael's Church of England School at High Street in Winterbourne.

1970s   The Rowlings move to Church Cottage, next to St. Luke's Church in Tutshill.

1974   September—Jo Rowling begins attending Tutshill Church of England Primary School, where she is made to sit in the "dumb row."

1976   September—Jo Rowling begins attending Wyedean Comprehensive School in Sedbury.

1979   Jo Rowling's aunt Marian gives her Jessica Mitford's *Hons and Rebels*. The book makes a lasting impression on Jo; she will later name her daughter after the author.

1980   July 31—Harry James Potter, Rowling's famous protagonist, is "born" to Lily Evans Potter and James Potter. The date is the same as Jo's fifteenth birthday.

Anne Rowling is diagnosed with multiple sclerosis.

1981   October 31—In Book One, Voldemort apparently kills Harry Potter's parents in an incident that leaves a scar on baby Harry's forehead. His attempt to kill baby Harry backfires, and he casts a spell on himself instead.

November 1—In Book One, Hagrid delivers infant Harry Potter to Dumbledore, who leaves the baby with the Dursleys on Privet Drive.

1982   Jo Rowling becomes head girl at Wyedean Comprehensive.

1983   April 23—Anne Rowling makes out her will to settle her affairs before her disease worsens.

Jo Rowling applies to Oxford University but is rejected. Many supporters claim the reason was that she had attended a public comprehensive school rather than an expensive private one.

Summer—Jo Rowling graduates from Wyedean Comprehensive Secondary School.

Fall—Jo Rowling begins study at University of Exeter, majoring in French and the classics (Greek and Roman studies).

1985–
1986   School year—Jo goes to Paris for Exeter's Year in France program. Teaches English. This is her first teaching experience.

1987   Spring—Jo Rowling graduates from University of Exeter.

1989   July 31—Daniel Radcliffe, the actor who portrays Harry Potter in the first two films, is born in London. He shares his birthday with both his famous character and Jo Rowling.

1990   June—Harry Potter arrives in Jo Rowling's imagination while she is daydreaming on a train ride from Manchester to London. She lacks her usual pen and paper and must remember everything she imagines until she gets home.

December 30—Anne Rowling dies of multiple sclerosis at age forty-five.

1991   July 31—In Book One, Harry Potter receives the letter from Albus Dumbledore, inviting him to attend Hogwarts School of Witchcraft and Wizardry. The date is the same as Jo's twenty-sixth birthday.

1992   Summer—Jo reportedly suffers a miscarriage of her first baby with Jorge Arantes.

August 28—Jorge Arantes reportedly proposes marriage to Jo Rowling.

October 16—Jo Rowling marries Jorge Alberto Rodrigues Arantes, a Portuguese television journalist, in a civil ceremony in Oporto, Portugal. Rowling wears black for the ceremony. In *Prisoner of Azkaban*, October 16th is also the date that Divination Professor Trelawney tells Lavender Brown the event she has been dreading will occur.

1993   July 27—Jo gives birth to a baby girl, Jessica. Jo names her after her favorite writer and activist role model, Jessica Mitford.

November 17—In a violent quarrel, Jorge throws Jo out on the street in Oporto, Portugal.

Christmas—Jo leaves Jorge, taking baby Jessica back to Britain and to her sister's house in Edinburgh, Scotland. In Jo's suitcase are Harry Potter manuscripts and notes.

1994   Jo Rowling shares Harry Potter with her sister, Di, who enjoys the story and encourages her sister to finish it.

Rowling begins writing at cafes while Jessica sleeps in a stroller next to her table. They scrape out a living on public assistance, about $105 per week.

1995   Jo Rowling finishes the first Harry Potter book and sends it to agent Christopher Little because she likes his name.

1997   February—Scottish Arts Council awards Jo Rowling $13,000 as an artist's grant in support of her work, a record amount for a children's author.

June—Rowling's first book, *Harry Potter and the Philosopher's Stone*, is published by Bloomsbury Publishers in Britain.

1998   July—Book Two, *Harry Potter and the Chamber of Secrets*, is published in Britain by Bloomsbury.

Book One is in published America, retitled *Harry Potter and the Sorcerer's Stone*.

1999   Book Three, *Harry Potter and the Prisoner of Azkaban*, is published in Britain by Bloomsbury.

2000   July 8—Jo Rowling rides Hogwarts Express replica train on a four-day tour across England to promote the release of Book Four, *Harry Potter and the Goblet of Fire*.

2001   November 4—The film *Harry Potter and the Sorcerer's Stone* premieres in London.

November 16–18—Harry Potter film breaks gross profits records for opening day and weekend in American theaters.

Rowling and her husband-to-be, Neil Murray, purchase Killiechassie House, a mansion in the Scottish countryside.

December 26—Jo marries Dr. Neil Murray, an anaesthetist, at Killiechassie House.

2002   March 20—Date for publication of Book Five, *Harry Potter and the Order of the Phoenix,* is pushed back from summer to autumn 2002, in an announcement by Nigel Newton of Bloomsbury Publishers. The delay was reportedly due to Rowling having not yet finished the manuscript. A later delay is indefinite.

March 24—The film *Harry Potter and the Sorcerer's Stone* is nominated for three Oscars from the Academy of Motion Pictures Arts and Sciences: Best Art Direction, Best Costume, and Best Original Score. It wins no award.

November 15—Second film by Warner Brothers, *Harry Potter and the Chamber of Secrets,* is released.

APPENDIX B   J. K. ROWLING'S AWARDS

Book 1 (Year 1)

Harry Potter and the Philosopher's Stone (*Harry Potter and the Sorcerer's Stone* in the United States), Bloomsbury, U.K., 1997; Scholastic, U.S. 1998. Cover illustrated by Thomas Taylor (U.K.); Mary GrandPré (U.S.). 309 pages.

Awards

Smarties Book Prize Gold Award, 1997; British Book Awards Children's Book of the Year, 1998; FCBG Children's Book Awards winner overall, 1998; Young Telegraph Paperback of the Year, 1998; Birmingham Cable Children's Book Award; Sheffield Children's Book Award; The Booksellers Association/The Bookseller Author of the Year, 1998; American Booksellers Book Award, 1999; Children's Book Prize 1999 of the "Jury of Young Readers" Vienna; Kinderboekwinkelprijs, 1999; Premio Cento per la Letteratura Infantile, 1998; Anne Spencer Libergh Prize in Children's Literature 1997–1998; Prix Sorciere, 1999; Prix Tam-Tam "Je bouquine," 1999; *School Library Journal* Best Book of the Year; American Library Association Notable Book and Best Book for Young Adults, 1998; *Publishers Weekly* Best Book of the Year; New York Public Library Best

Book of the Year; *Parenting* Magazine Book of the Year Award, 1998; Smithsonian Notable Books for Children; Borders Books Choice for 1999; *Booklist* Editors' Choice, 1998; shortlisted for the Carnegie Medal (commended), 1998; the *Guardian* Fiction Prize, 1998; Deutscher Jugendliteraturpreis, 1999.

Book 2 (Year 2)

Harry Potter and the Chamber of Secrets, Bloomsbury, U.K., 1998; Scholastic, U.S., 1999. Cover illustrated by Cliff Wright (U.K.); Mary GrandPré (U.S.). 341 pages.

Awards

Smarties Book Prize Gold Award, 1998; British Book Awards Children's Book of the Year, 1999; FCBG Children's Book Awards, 1999; Scottish Arts Council Children's Book Award, 1999; North East Book Award; North East Scotland Book Award; American Library Association Notable Book and Best Book for Young Adults, 1999; *Booklist* Editors' Choice, 1999; *School Library Journal* Best Book of the Year, 1999; shortlisted for the Whitbread Children's Book of the Year Award, 1999; Sheffield Children's Book Award; *Guardian* Fiction Prize, 1999; BA Author of the Year, 1999.

Book 3 (Year 3)

Harry Potter and the Prisoner of Azkaban. Bloomsbury, U.K., 1999; Scholastic, U.S., 1999. Cover illustrated by Cliff Wright (U.K.); Mary GrandPré (U.S.). 435 pages.

Awards

Whitbread Children's Book of the Year Award, 2000; British Book Awards Children's Author of the Year, 2000; Smarties Book Prize Gold Award, 1999; American Library Association Notable Book and Best Book for Young Adults, 2000; *Los Angeles Times* Best Book, 1999; *Booklist* Editors' Choice, 2000; shortlisted for the Carnegie Medal; BA Author of the Year, 2000; OBE for Services to Children's Literature, 2000.

Book 4 (Year 4)

Harry Potter and the Goblet of Fire. Bloomsbury, U.K., 2000; Scholastic, U.S., 2000. Cover illustrated by Giles Greenfield (U.K.); Mary GrandPré (U.S.). 734 pages.

Awards

Shortlisted for British Book Awards Children's Book of the Year, 2000; *Publishers Weekly* Best Children's Books of 2000; Smithsonian Notable Children's Books, 2000; Amazon.com Editors' Choice selection, ages 9–12; *Booklist* Editors' Choice, 2000; American Library Association Notable Children's Book, 2000; Honorary Doctorate Degree, Exeter University, 2000.

APPENDIX C   J. K. ROWLING'S READING

In interviews, J. K. Rowling has acknowledged or implied reading the books below, among others, as a child or an adult. Full citations of currently available editions of selected books from this list are included in the bibliography.

The American Way of Birth, Jessica Mitford
The American Way of Death, Jessica Mitford
The American Way of Death Revisited, Jessica Mitford
Black Beauty, Anna Sewell
Chronicles of Narnia, C. S. Lewis
Daughters and Rebels: An Autobiography, Jessica Mitford
Dictionary of Phrase and Fable, Ebenezer Cobham Brewer
Emma, Jane Austen
Faces of Philip: A Memoir of Philip Toynbee, Jessica Mitford
A Fine Old Conflict, Jessica Mitford
Grace Had an English Heart, Jessica Mitford
The Hobbit, J. R. R. Tolkien
Hons and Rebels, Jessica Mitford
Kind and Unusual Punishment, Jessica Mitford
The Little White Horse, Elizabeth Goudge
Little Women, Louisa May Alcott
The Lord of the Rings, Trilogy, J. R. R. Tolkien
Poison Penmanship: The Gentle Art of Muckraking, Jessica Mitford
Pride and Prejudice, Jane Austen

The Secret Garden, Frances Hodgson Burnett
A Tale of Two Cities, Charles Dickens
Thunderball, Ian Fleming
The Story of the Treasure Seekers, Edith Nesbit
Vanity Fair, William Thackeray
The Trial of Dr. Spock, the Rev. William Sloane Coffin, Jr., Michael Ferber, Mitchell Goodman, and Marcus Raskin, Jessica Mitford
Watership Down, Richard Adams
The Wind in the Willows, Kenneth Grahame
The Writers' and Artists' Yearbook (annual editions), published by A&C Black

APPENDIX D ORGANIZATIONS IMPORTANT TO J. K. ROWLING

Rowling's work before Harry Potter and her humanitarian efforts after the success of the series represent one of the hallmarks of her life. Below are key organizations she has supported with her time and/or major donations.

Amnesty International, UK
99–119 Rosebery Avenue
London EC1R 4RE
Phone: 020 7814 6200
Fax: 020 7833 1510
email: information@amnesty.org.uk
Website: http://www.amnesty.org.uk

Amnesty International, US
322 Eighth Avenue
New York, NY 10001
Phone: (212) 807-8400
Fax: (212) 627-1451
email: aimember@aiusa.org
Website: http://www.amnesty-usa.org/

Comic Relief, UK
Fifth Floor
89 Albert Embankment
London SE1 7TP
Phone: 020 7820 5555

Fax: 020 7820 5500
email: red@comicrelief.org.uk
Website: http://www.comicrelief.org.uk

Comic Relief, US
6404 Wilshire Boulevard #960
Los Angeles, CA 90048
Phone: (800) 323-5275
email: randy@comicrelief.org
Website: http://www.comicrelief.org

Multiple Sclerosis Society
MS National Centre
372 Edgware Road
Staples Corner
London NW2 6ND
Phone: 020 8438 0700
Website: http://www.mssociety.org.uk

National Multiple Sclerosis Society
733 Third Avenue
6th Floor
New York, NY 10017
Phone: (212) 986-3240 or (800) Fight MS (344-4867)
Fax: (212) 986-7981
Website: http://www.nationalmssociety.org

National Council for One Parent Families
255 Kentish Town Road
London NW5 2LX
Phone: 020 7428 5400
Fax: 020 7482 4851
email: info@oneparentfamilies.org.uk
Website: http://www.oneparentfamilies.org.uk

APPENDIX E   ADDRESSES FOR J.K. ROWLING

J.K. Rowling
c/o Bloomsbury Publishing Plc
38 Soho Square
London W1D 3HB
UNITED KINGDOM

J.K. Rowling
c/o Christopher Little Literary Agency
10 Eel Brook Studios
125 Moore Park Road
London SW6 4PS
UNITED KINGDOM

J.K. Rowling
c/o Scholastic Books, Inc.
557 Broadway
New York, NY 10012
USA

Websites

Bloomsbury (British publisher, Harry Potter)
http://www.bloomsburymagazine.com/harrypotter/
J.K. Rowling, author: http://www.jkrowling.com

Scholastic (American publisher, Harry Potter)
http://www.scholastic.com/harrypotter/

Warner Brothers (Harry Potter films)
http://www.harrypotter.warnerbros.com/

BIBLIOGRAPHY

WORKS BY J. K. ROWLING

Rowling, J. K. Foreword. *Families Just Like Us: The One Parent Families Good Book Guide*. London: Young Book Trust and National Council for One Parent Families, 2000.

———. *Harry Potter and the Chamber of Secrets* (Year 2). London: Bloomsbury, 1998.

——— *Harry Potter and the Chamber of Secrets* (Year 2). New York: Scholastic, 1998.

———. *Harry Potter and the Goblet of Fire* (Year 4). London: Bloomsbury, 2000.

———. *Harry Potter and the Goblet of Fire* (Year 4). New York: Scholastic, 2000.

———. *Harry Potter and the Order of the Phoenix* (Year 5). London: Bloomsbury, forthcoming.

———. *Harry Potter and the Order of the Phoenix* (Year 5). New York: Scholastic, forthcoming.

———. *Harry Potter and the Philosopher's Stone* (Year 1). London: Bloomsbury, 1997.

———. *Harry Potter and the Prisoner of Azkaban* (Year 3). London: Bloomsbury, 1999.

———. *Harry Potter and the Prisoner of Azkaban* (Year 3). New York: Scholastic, 1999.

———. *Harry Potter and the Sorcerer's Stone* (Year 1). New York: Scholastic, 1998.

———. "J. K. Rowling's diary." *Sunday Times* (London), July 26, 1998.

———. "Let me tell you a story." *Sunday Times* (London), May 21, 2000.

———. "The not especially fascinating life so far of J.K. Rowling." 1998. http://www.okukbooks.com/harry/rowling.htm.

Scamander, Newt [J.K. Rowling]. *Fantastic Beasts and Where to Find Them*. London: Bloomsbury and Obscurus Books, 2001.

———. *Fantastic Beasts and Where to Find Them*. New York: Scholastic and Obscurus Books, 2001.

Whisp, Kennilworthy [J.K. Rowling]. *Quidditch Through the Ages*. London: Bloomsbury and Whizzhard Books, 2001.

———. *Quidditch Through the Ages*. New York: Scholastic and Whizzhard Books, 2001.

AUDIO BOOKS AND MOVIES

Harry Potter and the Chamber of Secrets. Audio CD/cassettes [unabridged]. Performed by Stephen Fry (UK). BBC Audio (Spoken Word), 2000.

———. Performed by Jim Dale (USA). Bantam Books-Audio, 1999.

Harry Potter and the Goblet of Fire. Audio CD/cassettes [unabridged]. Performed by Stephen Fry (UK). BBC Audio (Spoken Word), 2001.

———. Performed by Jim Dale (USA). Bantam Books-Audio, 2000.

Harry Potter and the Prisoner of Azkaban. Audio CD/cassettes [unabridged]. Performed by Stephen Fry (UK). BBC Audio (Spoken Word), 2000.

———. Performed by Jim Dale (USA). Bantam Books-Audio, 2000.

Harry Potter and the Sorcerer's Stone. Audio CD/cassettes [unabridged]. Performed by Stephen Fry (UK). BBC Audio (Spoken Word), 1999.

———. Performed by Jim Dale (USA). Bantam Books-Audio, 1999.

———. Film, VHS, DVD/DVD-ROM. Directed by Christopher Columbus. Warner Bros., 2001.

BIOGRAPHY

Adler, Margot. Profile of J.K. Rowling. *All Things Considered*. National Public Radio, December 3, 1998.

Barker, Raffaella. "Harry Potter's mum." *Good Housekeeping*, October 2000.

Barnes and Noble chat with J.K. Rowling. October 20, 2000. http://www.hpnetwork.f2s.com/jkrowling/jkrbnchat.html.

Bethune, Brian. "The Rowling connection: How a young Toronto girl's story touched an author's heart." *Maclean's*, November 6, 2000: 92.

Egan, Kelly. "Potter author thrills 15,000: J.K. Rowling leads 'revolution.'" *The Ottawa Citizen*, October 25, 2000: A3.

Fraser, Lindsey. *Conversations with J.K. Rowling*. New York: Scholastic, Inc., 2001.

———. *Telling Tales: An Interview with J.K. Rowling*. London: Mammoth, 2000.

Gaines, Ann. *J.K. Rowling: A Real-Life Reader Biography* (elementary school level). Bear, DE: Mitchell Lane Publishers, Inc., 2002.

Gray, Paul. "Wild about Harry." *Time*, September 20, 1999.

Glaister, Dan. "Debut author and single mother sells children's book for £100,000." *The Guardian* (Manchester), July 8, 1997: 4.

"J.K. Rowling chat: May 4, 2000." http://www.geocities.com/harrypotter-fans /jkraolchat.html.

"J.K. Rowling chat transcript." October 2000. http://www.hpnetwork.f2s.com /jkraolchat.html.

"J.K. Rowling reads for the magic." *O Magazine*, January 2001: 150–151.

"J.K. Rowling's bookshelf." *O Magazine*, January 2001: 155.

Jones, Malcolm. "The Return of Harry Potter!" *Newsweek*, July 10, 2000: 52–60.

Judge, Elizabeth. "Rowling rejects Tory's family 'norm.'" *The Times* (London), December 6, 2000.

"Magic, mystery, and mayhem: An interview with J.K. Rowling." http://www .amazon.com/exec/obidos/ts/feature/6230/.

Mehren, Elizabeth. "Upward and onward toward book seven—her way." *Los Angeles Times*, October 25, 2000: E1.

National Press Club. Reading and question-and-answer session. October 20, 1999. Book–TV, C-SPAN2, November 6, 1999.

"Now it's Doctor Rowling." *Post and Courier* (Charleston, SC), July 15, 2000: 2A.

Power, Carla, with Shehnaz Suterwalla. "A literary sorceress." *Newsweek*, December 7, 1998: 7.

Ramirez, Michael. "Survivors." *Los Angeles Times*, July 14, 2000. Repr. http://cagle .slates.msn.com/news/harrypotter/main.asp.

The Rosie O'Donnell Show. Interview with J.K. Rowling. WB (Warner Bros.) Television Network, June 21, 1999.

"A Rowling Timeline." *Book*, May–June, 2000: 40–45.

Savill, Richard. "Harry Potter and the mystery of J.K.'s lost initial." *The Daily Telegraph* (London), July 19, 2000: 3.

Sayid, Ruki. "The Million-Hers; 50 Top Earning Women in the British Isles." *The Mirror*, October 18, 1999: 11.

Shapiro, Marc. *J.K. Rowling: The Wizard Behind Harry Potter*. New York: St. Martin's, 2000.

Smith, Sean. *J.K. Rowling: A Biography*. London: Michael O'Mara Books, Ltd., 2001.

Solomon, Evan. "J.K. Rowling interview." *Hot Type*. Canadian Broadcasting Corporation (CBC), July 2000. http://cbc.ca/programs/sites/hottype _rowlingcomplete.html.

Stahl, Lesley. Profile of J.K. Rowling. *60 Minutes*. CBS, September 12, 1999.

Steffens, Bradley. *J.K. Rowling* (People in the News Series). San Diego, CA: Lucent Books, 2002.

Transcript of J. K. Rowling's live interview on Scholastic.com, February 3, 2000. http://www.scholastic.com/harrypotter/author/transcript1.htm.

Trueland, Jennifer. "Author's ex-husband gets in on the Harry Potter act." *The Scotsman*, November 15, 1999: 3.

Walker, Andrew. "Edinburgh author is elated as America goes potty over Potter." *The Scotsman*, October 29, 1998: 7.

Weeks, Linton. "Charmed, I'm sure: The enchanting success story of Harry Potter's creator, J. K. Rowling." *Washington Post*, October 20, 1999: C1.

Weir, Margaret. "Of magic and single motherhood." *Salon*, March 31, 1999. http://www.salon.com/mwt/feature/1999/03/cov_31featureb.html.

CITED PRIMARY SOURCES

Austen, Jane. *Emma*. (1815). Oxford and New York: Oxford University Press, 1992.

———. *Mansfield Park*. (1814). New York: Penguin, 1996.

———. *Pride and Prejudice*. (1813) New York: Penguin, 1996.

Bambi. Walt Disney Productions. Film. 1962.

Baum, L. Frank. *The Wonderful Wizard of Oz*. (1900). New York: Oxford, 1997.

Brewer, Ebenezer Cobham, et. al. *The Dictionary of Phrase and Fable*, 16th ed. New York: HarperCollins, 2000.

Carroll, Lewis. *The Annotated Alice: Definitive Edition*. New York: W. W. Norton & Co., 2000.

Dahl, Roald. *Charlie and the Chocolate Factory*. (1964; revised 1973). New York: Alfred A. Knopf, 1983.

———. *James and the Giant Peach*. 1961. New York: Puffin Books, 1988.

Dickens, Charles. *A Tale of Two Cities*. (1859). New York: New American Library, 1997.

Fleming, Ian. *Thunderball*. New York: Viking Press, 1961.

Goudge, Elizabeth. *The Little White Horse*. (1946). Cutchogue, NY: Buccaneer Books, Inc., 2001.

Grahame, Kenneth. *The Wind in the Willows*. (1908). New York: Charles Scribner's Sons, 1983.

Hines, Barry. *A Kestral for a Knave* (1968).

———. *Kes*. Film based on Barry Hines's *A Kestral for a Knave*. (1969). by Ken Loach. Play adaptation by Lawrence Till.

Lewis, C. S. *Chronicles of Narnia*. (1950+). New York: Macmillan, 1988.

Mitford, Jessica. *Hons and Rebels*. (1960). London: Orion Books, Ltd., 2000.

Raskin, Ellen. *The Westing Game*. (1978). New York: Viking/Penguin, 1997.

Risom, Ole. *I Am a Bunny*. Illustrated by Richard Scarry. New York: Golden Books Publishing Company, Inc., 1963.

Scarry, Richard. *The Best Storybook Ever*. New York: Golden Books Publishing Company, Inc., 1968.

Sewell, Anna. *Black Beauty: The Autobiography of a Horse*. (1877). New York: Barnes & Noble Books, 1994.

Shakespeare, William. *King Lear*. New York: Penguin/Putnam, Inc., 1998.

———. *A Winter's Tale*. New York: Viking/Penguin, 1999.

Tolkien, J. R. R. *The Hobbit*. (1937). New York: Houghton Mifflin, 2002.

———. *The Lord of the Rings*. Trilogy (1954–1955). New York: Houghton Mifflin, 1994.

Yolen, Jane. *Wizard's Hall*. New York: Harcourt, Inc., 1991.

READING AND EDUCATION GUIDES

Beech, Linda Ward. *Scholastic Literature Guide: Harry Potter and the Chamber of Secrets by J. K. Rowling*. New York: Scholastic, 2000.

———. *Scholastic Literature Guide: Harry Potter and the Goblet of Fire by J. K. Rowling*. New York: Scholastic, 2000.

———. *Scholastic Literature Guide: Harry Potter and the Sorcerer's Stone by J. K. Rowling*. New York: Scholastic, 2000.

Colbert, David. *The Magical Worlds of Harry Potter: A Treasury of Myths, Legends, and Fascinating Facts*. Wrightsville Beach, NC: Lumina Press, LLC, 2001.

Kronzck, Allan Zola, and Elizabeth Kronzck. *The Sorcerer's Companion: A Guide to the Magical World of Harry Potter*. New York: Broadway Books, 2001.

Nel, Philip. *J. K. Rowling's Harry Potter Novels: A Reader's Guide*. New York: Continuum, 2001.

Schafer, Elizabeth D. *Beacham's Sourcebooks for Teaching Young Adult Fiction: Exploring Harry Potter*. Osprey, FL: Beacham Publishing Corp., 2000.

REVIEWS AND CRITICISM

Abanes, Richard. *Harry Potter and the Bible: The Menace Behind the Magick*. Colorado Springs, CO: Christian Publishing, Inc. (Horizon Books), 2001.

Acocella, Joan. "Under the spell." *The New Yorker*, July 31, 2000: 74–78.

Ahuja, Anjana. "Harry Potter's novel encounter," *London Times*, June 27, 2000.

Alderson, Brian. "A View from the island: Harry Potter, Dido Twite, and Mr. Beowulf." *The Horn Book* 76 (May/June, 2000): 349.

"The American way of giving." *The Economist*, January 25, 2001.

Bernstein, Richard. "Examining the reality of the fantasy in the Harry Potter stories." *New York Times* (December 2, 1999): B1.

Blacker, Terence. "Why does everyone like Harry Potter?" *The Independent* (London), July 13, 1999: 4.

Bloom, Harold. "Can 35 million book buyers be wrong? Yes." *Wall Street Journal*, July 11, 2000: A26.

Blume, Judy. "Is Harry Potter evil?" *New York Times*, October 22, 1999.

Bradman, Tony. "Mayhem wherever he flits." *London Times Literary Supplement*, 22 (December 2000).

Briggs, Julia. "Fighting the forces of evil." *London Times Literary Supplement*, 22 (December 2000).

Bruce, Ian S. "Wizard read lives up to hype." *Sunday Herald* (UK), July 9, 2000: 3.

Buchanan, Ben. *My Year with Harry Potter: How I Discovered My Own Magical World*. New York: Lantern Books, 2001.

Cochrane, Lynne. "Harry's home." *Sunday Times* (London), July 2, 2000.

Cohen, Whitaker E. "Hands off Harry!" Letter to the editor, *New Yorker*, October 18–25, 1999: 16.

Collins, Gail. "An ode to July." *New York Times*, July 11, 2000: A31.

———. "Rudy's identity crisis." *New York Times*, April 14, 2000.

Cowell, Alan. "All aboard the Harry Potter promotional express; an author's promotional juggernaut keeps rolling on." *New York Times*, July 10, 2000.

Cox, Rose. "Harry Potter books inspire new love for literature." *Anchorage Daily News*, January, 26, 2002.

Craig, Amanda. "Harry Potter and the Prisoner of Azkaban." *New Statesman*, July 12, 1999: 74.

Crittenden, Daniele. "Boy meets book." *Wall Street Journal*, November 26, 1999: W13.

Demetrious, Danielle. "Harry and the source of inspiration." *Daily Telegraph* (London), July 1, 2000: 3.

Dirda, Michael. "Harry Potter and the Chamber of Secrets." *Washington Post*, July 4, 1999.

Donahue, Deirdre. "'Goblet of Fire' burns out." *USA Today*, July 10, 2000: 1D.

———. "Harry Potter's simplicity lures kids of all ages." *USA Today*, June, 9, 2000: 10B.

Dowd, Maureen. "Dare speak his name." *New York Times*, October 2000: 15.

———. "Veni, vidi, Voldemort." *New York Times*, December, 9, 2001.

Dubail, Jean. "Finding children's magic in world of Harry Potter." *The Plain Dealer* (Cleveland), June 13, 1999: 10I.

Dunbar, Robert. "Simply wizard." *The Irish Times*, July 17, 1999.

———. "Volumes of choices for the holidays." *The Scotsman*, June 28, 1997: 15.

Friedman, Thomas L. "Lebanon and the goblet of fire." *New York Times*, July 11, 2000: 31.

Galloway, Jim. "Harry Potter: School lets hero off hook." *Atlanta Journal and Constitution*. October 13, 1999: 1B.

Gibbons, Fiachra. "Harry Potter banned from paper's bestseller list." *The Guardian*, July 17, 1999: Home, 6.

Gibbs, Nancy. "Harry is an old soul." *Time*, December 25, 2000.

Gilson, Nancy. "Sorcerer's Stone looks like a real page-turner." *Columbus Dispatch*. September 17, 1998: Weekender, p. 20.

Gish, Kimbra Wilder. "Hunting down Harry Potter: An exploration of religious concerns about children's literature." *Horn Book*, May–June, 2000: 263–271.

Gleick, Elizabeth. "The wizard of Hogwarts." *Time*, April 12, 1999.

Gleick, Peter H. "Harry Potter, minus a certain flavour." *New York Times*, July 10, 2000: A25.

Grybaum, Gail A. "The secrets of Harry Potter." *San Francisco Jung Institute Library Journal* 19, no. 4 (2001): 17–48.

Hainer, Cathy. "Second time's still a charm." *USA Today*, May 27, 1999: 1D.

———. "Third time's another charmer for 'Harry Potter.'" *USA Today*, September 8, 1999: 1D.

Hall, Dinah. "Children's books: Junior fiction." *Sunday Telegraph*, July 27, 1997: 14.

———. "Children's books for summer: Fiction." *Sunday Telegraph*, July 19, 1998: Books, 12.

Harrington-Lueker, Donna. "'Harry Potter lacks for true heroines." *USA Today*, July 11, 2000: 17A.

Hattenstone, Simon. "Harry, Jessie and me." *The Guardian*, July 8, 2000: Weekend, 32.

Hensher, Philip. "Harry Potter, give me a break." *The Independent* (London), January 25, 2000: 1.

Holt, Karen Jenkins. "Spreading the Potter magic." *Brill's Content*, April, 2001: 98.

Hopkinson, Victoria. "Walks on the wild side and on the mild side." *Financial Times* (London), October 4, 1997: 6.

Iyer, Pico. "The playing fields of Hogwarts." *New York Times*, October 10, 1999: Book Review, 39.

Jerome, Helen M. "Welcome back, Potter." *Book*, May–June, 2000: 40–45.

Johnson, Daniel. "The monster of children's books J.K. Rowling shows originality and imagination: Why then has she inspired such vitriol?" *Daily Telegraph* (London), January 29, 2000: 24.

Johnson, Sarah. "First review: New Harry Potter's 'a cracker.'" *The Times* (London), July 8, 2000: 1–2.

———. "Go for good writing." *The Times* (London), August 23, 1997.

———. "Just wild about Harry." *The Times* (London), April 23, 1999.

Johnstone, Anne. "Fun is brought to book." *The Herald* (Glasgow), July 4, 1998: 14.

———. "Happy ending, and that's for beginners." *The Herald* (Glasgow), June 24, 1997: 15.

———. "A kind of magic." *The Herald* (Glasgow), July 8, 2000: *Saturday Magazine*, 8–12.

Judah, Hettie. "Harry is pure magic." *The Herald* (Glasgow), July 15, 1999.

Kantor, Jodi, and Judith Shulevitz. "The new Harry: Riotous, rushed, and remarkable." *Slate*, July 10–13, 2000. http://slate.msn.com/code/Book-Club/BookClub.asp ?Show=7/10/00&idMessage=5648&idBio=183.

King, Stephen. "Wild about Harry." *New York Times*, July 23, 2000: Book Review, 13–14.

Kipen, David. "J. K. Rowling's fantasy series hits an awkward teenage phase with 'Goblet.'" *San Francisco Chronicle*, July 10, 2000.

Levi, Jonathan. "Pottermania." *Los Angeles Times*, July 16, 2000: Book Review, 1.

Levine, Arthur A., with Doreen Carvajal. "Why I paid so much." *New York Times*, October 13, 1999: C14.

Lively, Penelope. "Harry's in robust form, although I'm left bug-eyed." *The Independent* (London), July 13, 2000: 5.

Lockerbie, Catherine. "Just wild about Harry." *The Scotsman*, July 9, 1998: 12.

———. "Magical mystery tour de force." *The Scotsman*, July 10, 1999: 11.

Loer, Stephanie. "Harry Potter is taking publishing world by storm." *Boston Globe*, January 3, 1999: M10.

Lurie, Alison. "Not for muggles." *New York Review of Books*, December 16, 1999. http://www.nybooks.com/nyrev/WWWfeatdisplay.cgi?19991216006.

Macdonald, Hugh. "Potter's deal … or the importance of being Harry." *The Herald* (Glasgow), July 8, 2000: Saturday Magazine, 8–12.

Macguire, Gregory. "Lord of the golden snitch." *New York Times*, September 5, 1999: Book Review, 12.

Macmonagle, Niall. "The season of the wizard." *The Irish Times*, July 15, 2000: 69.

Maslin, Janet. "At last, the wizard gets back to school." *New York Times*. July 10, 2000: E1.

McCrum, Robert. "Plot, plot, plot that's worth the weight." *The Observer* 9 (July 2000).

Mutter, John, and Jim Milliot. "Harry Potter and the weekend of fiery sales." *Publishers Weekly*, July 17, 2000: 76.

Neal, Connie. *What's a Christian to Do with Harry Potter?* Colorado Springs, CO: WaterBrook Press, 2001.

Ohman, Jack. "Gore-Potter 2000." Repr. *Washington Post*, National Weekly Edition, no. 24 (July 2000): 27.

Parravano, Martha P. "J. K. Rowling, Harry Potter and the Chamber of Secrets." *Horn Book*, July–August, 1999: 74.

Phelan, Laurence. "Books: Christmas dystopia: Parents, ghosts, the future, bullying and lemonade." *The Independent* (London), December 6, 1998: 12.

Prynn, Jonathan. "Potter to join Pooh and classics." *The Evening Standard* (London), October 6. 1999: 23.

Radosh, Daniel. "Why American kids don't consider Harry Potter an insufferable prig." *New Yorker*, September 20, 1999: 54, 56.

Rose, Matthew, and Emily Nelson. "Potter cognoscenti all know a muggle when they see one." *Wall Street Journal*, October 18, 2000: A1, A10.

Rosenberg, Liz. "A foundling boy and his corps of wizards." *Boston Globe*, November 1, 1998: L2.

———. "Harry Potter's back again." *Boston Globe*, July 18, 1999: K3.

———. "Making much of memories." *Boston Globe*, September 19, 1999: H2.

Rustin, Susanna. "They're all just wild about Harry." *Financial Times* (London), April 22, 2000: 9.

Safire, William. "Besotted with Potter." *New York Times*, January 27, 2000: A27.

Sawyer, Kem Knapp. "Orphan Harry and his Hogwarts mates work their magic stateside." *St. Louis Post-Dispatch*, June 13, 1999: F12.

Schoefer, Christine. "Harry Potter's Girl Trouble." *Salon.com* (January 23, 2000), 1.

Sutton, Roger. "Potter's Field." *Horn Book*, September–October 1999: 500–501.

Taylor, Alan. "We all know about the hype but is J. K. Rowling really up with the greats?" *Scotland on Sunday*, July 11, 1999: 15.

Treneman, Ann. "Harry and me." *The Times* (London), June 30, 2000.

Tucker, Nicholas. "The rise and rise of Harry Potter." *Children's Literature in Education*, vol. 30, no. 4 (December 1999): 221–234.

"Turning a page at the Book Review." *The New York Times*, Fall 2000: Inside, 1–3.

"U.K.'s number one bestseller, 'Harry Potter and the Sorcerer's Stone,' tops bestseller charts in U.S." *Business Wire*, December 7, 1998.

Wasserman, Dan. "I can already see how it ends—the dark forces win." *Washington Post*, National Weekly Edition, No. 24 (July 2000): 28.

"We're off to see the wizards." *Nickelodeon*, October 2001: 52–54.

Will, George F. "Harry Potter: A wizard's return." *Washington Post*, July 4, 2000: A19.

Winerip, Michael. "Children's books." *New York Times Book Review*, February 14, 1999. http://www.nytimes.com/books/99/02/14/reviews/990214.14childrt .html.

Wynee-Jones, Tim. "Harry Potter and the blaze of publicity: On the whole, the junior wizard deserves it all." *The Ottawa Citizen*, July 16, 2000: C16.

Zipes, Jack. "The virtue (and vice) of stolid sameness: Harry sells millions, not because he's new, but because he's as old as King Arthur." *The Ottawa Citizen*, February 4, 2001: C15. Repr. from Zipes's *Sticks and Stones: The Trou-*

blesome Success of Children's Literature from Slovenly Peter to Harry Potter. New York: Routledge, 2001.

———. "The phenomenon of Harry Potter, or why all the talk?" ch. 9, p. 170–189, in *Sticks and Stones: The Troublesome Success of Children's Literature from Slovenly Peter to Harry Potter.* New York: Routledge, 2001.

Zipp, Yvonne. "Harry Potter swoops into great adventures." *Christian Science Monitor,* January 14, 1999: 19.

———. "Swooping to stardom." *Christian Science Monitor,* June 17, 1999: 19.

RESPONSES FROM YOUNG PEOPLE

Adler, Bill, ed. *Kids' Letters to Harry Potter from Around the World.* New York: Carroll & Graf Publishers, Inc., 2001.

Buchanan, Ben. *My Year with Harry Potter: How I Discovered My Own Magical World.* New York: Lantern Books, 2001.

Moore, Sharon, ed. *Harry Potter, You're the Best! A Tribute from Fans the World Over.* New York: St. Martin's, 2001.

RELATED SOURCES

Aaronvitch, David. "Harry Potter and the menace of global capitalism." *The Independent,* September 28, 2000. http://www.independent.co.uk/enjoyment/Books/Reviews/200009/thursbook280900.shtml.

Anderson, Nick. "Reality T.V." *Louisville Courier-Journal,* July 9, 2000. Repr. http://cagle.slate.msn.com/news/harrypotter/harry4.asp.

Barnes, Julian E. "Dragons and flying brooms: Mattel shows off its line of Harry Potter toys." *New York Times,* March 1, 2000: C1. http://www.nytimes.com/2001/03/01/business/01ADCO.html?pagewanted=all&0301inside.

Borges, Jorge Luis, with Margarita Guerrero. *The Book of Imaginary Beings.* New York: Dutton, 1969.

Browne, Bob. "Hi and Lois." Syndicated cartoon: March 19, 2001.

Campbell, Joseph. *The Hero with a Thousand Faces.* Princeton: Princeton University Press, 1968.

Carey, Joanna. "Who hasn't met Harry?" February 16, 1999. http://www.guardianunlimited.co.uk/Archive/Article/0,4273,3822242,00.html [August 16, 1999].

Clute, John, and John Grant. *The Encyclopedia of Fantasy.* New York: St. Martin's, 1999.

Conley, Darby. "Get Fuzzy." Syndicated cartoon: June 22, 2001.

Cowell, Alan. "Investors and children alike give rave reviews to Harry Potter books." *New York Times*, October 18, 1999. http:/www.nytimes.com /library/books/101899harry-potter.html.

Guiley, Rosemary Ellen. *The Encyclopedia of Witches and Witchcraft*. New York: Facts on File, 1999.

"Harry Potter books spark rise in satanism among children." *The Onion*, July 2000. http://www.theonion.com/onion3625/harry_potter.html.

Johnston, Lynn. "For Better or for Worse." Syndicated cartoon: August 1, 2000.

———. "For Better or for Worse." Syndicated cartoon: January 21, 2001.

Keane, Jeff, and Bil Keane. "Family Circus." Syndicated cartoon: October 29, 2000.

———. "Family Circus." Syndicated cartoon: October 31, 2000.

———. "Family Circus." Syndicated cartoon: December 31, 2000.

Keane, Bil. "Family Circus." Syndicated cartoon: April 9, 2000.

Nigg, Joseph. *The Book of Fabulous Beasts: A Treasury of Writings from Ancient Times to the Present*. New York: Oxford UP, 1999.

Ogden, Tom. *Wizards and Sorcerers: From Abracadabra to Zoroaster*. New York: Facts on File, 1977.

Phillips, Mark. "Pure magic." *CBS Sunday Morning*, September 26, 1999.

Pond, Steve. "Prince Harry." *TV Guide*, October 27–November 2, 2001: 20–30.

"Scholastic joins J.K. Rowling to publish two Harry Potter–inspired books for charity." Press Release, November 20, 2000. http://www.scholastic.com /aboutscholastic/news/press00/press_11.20.00.htm.

Schultz, Charles. "Peanuts." Syndicated cartoon: November 8, 1999.

Scott, A.O., and Polly Schulman. "Is Harry Potter the new Star Wars?" *Slate*, August 1999: 23–26. http://www.slates.com/code/BookClub/BookClub .asp?Show = 8/23/99&idMessag=3472&idBio=111.

"Something About Harry." *Vanity Fair*, October 2001: 300–321.

"What if Quidditch, the enchanted sport of wizards and witches featured in the Harry Potter books, were regulated by the NCAA?" *Sports Illustrated*, August 21, 2000: 33.

Williams, Geoff. "Harry Potter and … the trials of growing a business … the rewards of independence and ownership." *Entrepreneur*, February 2001: 62–65.

Willis, Roy. *Dictionary of World Myth*. London: Duncan Baird, 1995.

Willis, Scott. "Could you turn that down? I'm trying to read!" *San Jose Mercury News*, July 12, 2000. Repr. http://eagle.slate.msn.com/news/harrypotter /harry9.asp.

Young, Dean, and Denis Lebrun. "Blondie." Syndicated cartoon: December 4, 2000.

WEBSITES

Vander Ark, Steve. "Harry Potter Lexicon." http://www.i2k.com/~svderark
    /lexicon/index.html.
Bloomsbury (British publisher, Harry Potter): http://www.bloomsburymagazine
    .com/harrypotter/ J. K. Rowling, author: http://www.jkrowling.com.
Scholastic (American publisher, Harry Potter): http://www.scholastic.com
    /harrypotter/.
Warner Brothers (Harry Potter films): http://www.harrypotter.warnerbros.com.

INDEX

About the Author

CONNIE ANN KIRK is a writer and scholar who specializes in children's literature, American literature, and Emily Dickinson. She teaches English at Mansfield University in Pennsylvania and is the editor of the *Encyclopedia of American Children's and Young Adult Literature*, forthcoming from Greenwood Press. Ms. Kirk lives with her husband and two sons in upstate New York. She makes a donation from this biography's proceeds to Comic Relief.